Writing the Traditional ECQs and the
New Five-Page Senior Executive Service Federal Resume

The New SES Application

KATHRYN TROUTMAN
DIANE HUDSON BURNS

Foreword by Paul Thompson
Retired from Office of Personnel Management, Executive Resources

The Resume Place, Inc.

Federal Career Publishers

89 Mellor Avenue, Baltimore, MD 21228

Phone: (888) 480-8265

www.resume-place.com

Email: resume@resume-place.com

Printed in the United States of America

Copyright © 2011 by Kathryn Troutman

ISBN: 978-0-9824190-4-5

Publication Team

Developmental Editor: Emily Troutman and Paulina Chen

Cover and Interior Page Design: Paulina Chen

Curriculum Development, Exercises, and Design Contributions: Emily Troutman and Susan Custard

OPM SES Consultant and Contributor: Paul Thompson

Proofreader: Pamela Sikora

Table of Contents

Acknowledgments: Kathryn Troutman

First, I am remembering and thanking Edward J. (Ned) Lynch for his years of inspiring SES ECQ and executive federal resume writing, teaching lessons, and some of the original copy for the ECQ Writing Guide. Ned Lynch worked for The Resume Place during the Clinton years (after working for President Bush, both 41 and 43). Through his work with us, hundreds of executives received Ned's inspiring writing and advice for their ECQs and SES careers. Ned was a senior policy analyst for the Civil Service Subcommittee and Department of Immigration.

Ned wrote the first version of the ECQ Writing Guide, the original document on which we based this book. Further editions were updated and added by my daughter, Emily Troutman, who created the ECQ Writing Guide for training throughout government agencies. The ECQ mapping exercise, ECQ keyword lists, and Writer's Inspiration were all field-tested by aspiring executives across government.

Thank you to Susan Custard, who was a long-time SES writer, consultant, and SES trainer for The Resume Place, for her contributions to the updates of our ECQ Writing Guide exercises. And thanks as well to my co-author, Diane Hudson Burns, who has now contributed to this expanded version of The New SES Application. The new book includes more lessons that are critical to serious SES candidates.

Thank you to Paul Thompson, retired Office of Personnel Management Senior Policy Analyst, for his information about the transformation to the five-page SES federal resume. And finally, thanks to Tim Cannon, who has brought the SES ECQ behavior-based interview alive in our classes.

Diane Hudson Burns

It has been a delight to compose SES resumes and ECQ essays for my clients, provide one-on-one coaching to develop leadership stories and prepare clients for SES interviews, and deliver group training for scores of very talented senior level government, military transition, and non-government (corporate) employees during the past 15 years (and some additional 10 years of developing senior level KSAs and federal resume packages). The materials here are the culmination of years of work with SES applicants—many of whom have reached their aspirations and moved into SES.

I am grateful for the opportunity to train alongside Kathryn Troutman and Paul Thompson, and now collaborate on this definitive guide to writing the varied and complex SES and ECQ resumes/application packages, and prepare candidates for the SES application process and structured interview.

Foreword

Kathryn Troutman's latest work comes at a time of great uncertainty in the federal government, probably the greatest I've witnessed since coming to Washington over 30 years ago. Not only are civil servants confronting the first salary freeze in memory, there's also a sense that the rules of the road for federal employees may be shifting in some fundamental and permanent way.

Perhaps it is not a promising time, then, to be looking for a career as an executive in the federal government, as readers of this book are likely to be. Yet, the numbers tell a different story. Membership in the Senior Executive Service has reached almost historic highs, surpassing 7,500. While the SES count will fluctuate as missions change and particular agencies staff up or draw down, there is good reason to believe that a vital and even a relatively numerous SES corps will be seen not as a problem, but as a necessary part of the solution to the challenges facing our nation.

This was certainly the message conveyed to SES members on February 18, 2011, by Deputy Director for Management Jeffrey Zients of the Office of Management and Budget and Director John Berry of the Office of Personnel Management (OPM), in their memorandum announcing the President's Management Council's (PMC) SES initiative. Their memo states, "[T]he best organizations know that especially in challenging economic times, investing in their senior executives pays off," and goes on to describe just what kind of investment they have in mind.

The initiative calls for enhanced SES professional development, improved performance management, and an expanded and diversified executive talent pipeline for the government. It follows in the wake of studies and other work from government-focused think tanks like the Partnership for Public Service identifying the strengths and the weaknesses of the SES, and emphasizing the need to improve its effectiveness.

Clearly, then, whatever changes may be in the offing for how the government does business, effective, dedicated leadership is in demand now more than ever—and Ms. Troutman's detailed roadmap of the recondite and often confusing SES selection process could hardly have come at a better time.

The book provides both the government insider and the outside candidate what he or she needs to know to compete for these difficult-to-land positions. As founder of The Resume Place, perhaps the premier source of federal job application assistance, Ms. Troutman knows how to help talented executives compete successfully for SES jobs. She can provide unique insights into how to write effective and persuasive narrative statements on the Executive Core Qualifications (ECQs), the primary basis for selections to the career SES.

She has also incorporated important and timely advice on how to write an effective SES resume, the government's newest method for applying for SES positions. The resume-based method was first piloted by OPM in 2008 as a less time-consuming, more applicant-friendly method to attract seasoned executives from outside government to the SES. The pilot succeeded in attracting more applicants for SES positions, and this approach has now been taken up as part of the PMC SES initiative as a way to tap the best and the brightest executive talent from around the country.

Whatever application method is involved, Kathryn Troutman's book will surely help bring talented executives from all sectors to the SES by familiarizing them with the SES hiring process, in all its facets. In that sense, her work is an outstanding example of public-private partnership—lending her entrepreneurial spirit and vast reservoir of expertise to the government's own efforts to build a better SES for the future.

I commend her efforts, and I commend this book to you as an aspiring member of the SES. May your search lead to great professional fulfillment for you—and great benefit for our country in these challenging times.

Paul Thompson
Retired Civil Servant
Human Resources Management Consultant

> "[Kathryn's] work is an outstanding example of public-private partnership—lending her entrepreneurial spirit and vast reservoir of expertise to the government's own efforts to build a better SES for the future."

Introduction

Attaining a position with the Senior Executive Service (SES) may be a culmination of many years of leadership experience gained in corporate America; or climbing the ladder through civil service, being groomed for SES—perhaps even completing an SES candidate development program.

It may even be a lifelong dream, as one of my clients recently said to me after I worked with her to write her Executive Core Qualifications (ECQs) and she received two SES offers: "You helped me transform my ECQs into a superb package. You also helped me attain a personal goal. I have been dreaming of this moment for 25 years. Thank you again for your professionalism, superb expertise, guidance, and perseverance. I could not have done it without you."

The SES is seeking candidates who bring unique and productive solutions to address serious issues in our government today, and who have the vision and forethought to anticipate the needs, challenges, and issues of tomorrow. SES candidates must demonstrate passion and initiative with an ability to motivate, inspire, and lead people to embrace change and new ideas, while increasing productivity and driving results. Those selected for SES positions are capable of managing resources (funds and human capital), integrating technological advancements into government activities, and tapping the expertise of coalitions to ensure the sharing of information and networking across far-reaching organizational and international boundaries.

The SES application package with executive federal resume and ECQs (or the five-page resume-based SES application) is the pinnacle of career search documents—a "super resume," if you will—fully articulating a career history by recounting top-level leadership accomplishments through storytelling using the Challenge-Context-Action-Result (CCAR) model. The application package is just part of a process to attain SES—a process that includes clearly conveying one's career history in a well-expressed, persuasive, and powerful resume and ECQ/TQ essays, thorough analysis of the requirements of a position (including how to apply for a position), a structured/ behavior-based interview, possible additional assessments or interviews, and reference checks.

This book was written in a user-friendly, systematic manner to help you understand the nature of the SES, the process of applying for SES positions, and the proper way to develop and write your SES/ECQ application and prepare for the interview process, with a target of helping you reach your aspiration of attaining an SES position or positioning yourself to work toward your ultimate goal of reaching SES.

Best wishes for continued career success!

Diane Hudson Burns
Co-Author, The New SES Application

For more than 40 years, The Resume Place has set the standard in both private industry and federal employment services and education. I started the business on K Street in Washington, DC, just a young woman with a typewriter, writing resumes for local law students.

Over the years, I have watched the ebb and flow of presidents and political parties, rules and regulations, and tools and trends. Through our services alone, The Resume Place has helped more than 100,000 people seek meaningful, successful careers. I've written and published eight books. With my partner company, the Federal Career Training Institute, we've trained thousands of career counselors using my popular "Ten Steps to a Federal Job" method.

Despite this expertise, preparing an executive federal application remains a difficult task. We can gear up with the right information and insider knowledge—but then we must write.

The new SES application asks candidates to write about themselves with more clarity, precision, and vision than ever before. Baby Boomers are retiring and the federal government will need new leaders. But candidates to the Senior Executive Service still face stiff competition and a complex hiring process.

The New SES Application is based on our Executive Core Qualifications writing guide, which was designed and developed over the past ten years. We used the guide as a handout in our executive career classes taught in numerous agencies including NASA, Health and Human Services, the Environmental Protection Agency, and across the Department of Defense.

After many demands for an SES book, we finally expanded and refined the guide to share with the general public. To begin, we ask candidates to make a brief list of their Top Ten Career Accomplishments. Then we map those accomplishments across federal executive competencies: Leading Change, Leading People, Results Driven, Business Acumen, and Building Coalitions.

From that outline, candidates are able to expand on their accomplishments using the storytelling method required by the Office of Personnel Management: Challenge, Context, Action, and Result. Our goal is to break down the process into manageable pieces and help you identify your most competitive career accomplishments. We also include instructions, strategies, and samples to adapt to federal agencies' differing length and style requirements for applications.

The book shares the cumulative expertise of my writing staff, trainers, consultants, and clients. As with all of my books, you can expect that the samples are real (though fictionalized for anonymity) and the resumes landed jobs.

The days of the typewriter are over. The law students, accountants, and myriad civil service employees who came to The Resume Place years ago are now stepping up to become today's leaders. Whether you're coming from private industry, the armed forces, or inside the Beltway, we're ready to guide you on your way to the top. I'm proud to be along with you for the ride.

Sincerely,

Kathryn Troutman

Founder and Owner of The Resume Place and the Federal Career Training Institute

ECQ: LEADING PEOPLE
Executive VP Overcomes Leadership Challenges

"Empowered a diverse HQ staff with low morale; gained trust and energized a very talented management team and their direct-reports to exceed their potential. The management team handled their direct-reports in a very hierarchical, depreciative manner, resulting in many complaints and personnel turbulence. To establish the new leadership team, I scheduled an off-site meeting. I directed that the meeting be prepared and conducted by the new leadership team, who presented their proposals to senior management. This successful meeting institutionalized the new leadership construct and I achieved an enduring transformation to a leadership culture of inclusion, empowerment, and teamwork. The Region showed markedly improved morale and reduced personnel turbulence. "

Read the entire five-page SES federal resume in Judy Johnson's case study starting on page 148.

Chapter One

SES Basics

About the Senior Executive Service (SES)

The Senior Executive Service is composed of the men and women charged with bringing about the continuing transformation of government. These leaders possess an array of well-honed executive skills and share a broad vision of government and a firm commitment to effective public service.

Members of the SES serve in key positions at the highest levels of their agencies, just below the top presidential appointees. SES members are the major link between these appointees and their agencies' career workforce. In this capacity, they manage and oversee nearly every government activity in approximately 75 federal agencies.

Are SES Positions Available?

Nearly two million people work for the federal government, excluding the U.S. Postal Service. Of these, approximately 7,500, or 0.4%, are in the SES. With an average age of 53, about roughly half of all SES members are eligible to retire within the next three years. This means that there is no shortage of opportunities for joining the SES in the near future. As many as 1,000 positions open up for new SES members in a year, and these can be found in virtually every state across the country, though the majority are located in or around Washington, DC.

Opportunities for women and minorities in the SES have improved in recent years. As of 2010, more than 30% of SES members were women, and more than 17% were members of ethnic minorities.

How to Find SES Vacancies

All SES vacancies are advertised on the Office of Personnel Management's (OPM) USAJOBS website: www.usajobs.gov. From this site, you can browse for SES vacancy announcements and submit your applications.

SES Salary Information

The following table shows the range of salaries for SES members for 2011. SES members are not eligible for locality pay adjustments.

View this table at: http://www.opm.gov/oca/11tables/html/es.asp.

Other pay tables for executive and senior level federal employees can be found at: http://www.opm.gov/oca/11tables/indexSES.asp.

U.S. OFFICE OF PERSONNEL MANAGEMENT
Recruiting, Retaining and Honoring a World-Class Workforce to Serve the American People

Advanced Search | Go

Salaries & Wages

SALARY TABLE NO. 2011-ES

RATES OF BASIC PAY FOR MEMBERS OF THE SENIOR EXECUTIVE SERVICE (SES)

RATES FROZEN AT 2010 LEVELS

EFFECTIVE JANUARY 2011

Structure of the SES Pay System	Minimum	Maximum
Agencies with a Certified SES Performance Appraisal System	119554	179700
Agencies without a Certified SES Performance Appraisal System	119554	165300

. *Salaries and Wages*
. *Compensation Administration Home Page*

What Are the Differences Between SES, ST, and SL Positions?

Senior Executive Service (SES) positions are above GS-15 or equivalent and involve one or more of the criteria set forth in the United States Code (5 USC 3132), such as directing the work of an organization and monitoring progress toward organizational goals.

Scientific and professional (ST) positions are competitive service positions above the GS-15 level involving high-level research and development.

Senior level (SL) positions are also above the GS-15 level but usually do not meet the SES criteria and do not involve the research and development responsibilities of ST positions. SL positions may be in either the competitive or excepted service.

SES Federal Candidate Development Program (CDP)

The federal government offers an SES Candidate Development Program, based on the five Executive Core Qualifications (ECQs), to foster future federal agency leadership and prepare candidates for immediate entry into SES. This 12-month program is available by competition (from four agencies) for GS-15/equivalents. The model includes feedback-intensive mentoring and networking components to further assist candidates in their developmental journey to seek SES.

There is good news for candidates who successfully complete the program and obtain certification by an SES Qualifications Review Board (QRB)—they may be selected for an SES position anywhere in the federal government without further competition. As part of their leadership journey, GS-13s and 14s may want to include the CDP in their professional development plan target for when they attain the GS-15 level.

Executive Core Qualifications (ECQs)

ECQs are executive level "knowledge, skills, and abilities" (KSAs) focused on the 28 leadership competencies identified by OPM.

ECQ narratives are generally more complex than other KSA statements because they reflect the leadership competencies (behaviors) that OPM has determined as critical for successful performance in an executive level position.

History of ECQs

The ECQs, and their underlying competencies, are based on extensive research into the attributes of successful executives in both the private and public sectors, including: a behavioral indicators study to update the executive competencies identified through a 1991 OPM survey of 10,000 supervisors, managers, and executives; an extensive review of private sector competency models and current literature on executive competencies; and focus groups of executives from a cross section of agencies and occupations.

Federal agencies, private sector representatives, and the National Academy of Public Administration all played a role in developing the ECQs. Members of the SES and the Senior Executives Association were encouraged to review an early draft and share their comments.

The first set of executive qualifications, established at the beginning of the SES, remained in effect until the mid-1990s, when they were completely overhauled to reflect developments in executive competencies over time. OPM issued the first version of the current ECQs in September 1997, as a result of the rapidly-changing management environment and the need to focus increasingly on leadership and the ability to drive change. The original ECQs were revalidated in 2006, with relatively minor changes.

ECQs and Executive Leadership

The Executive Core Qualifications are required for entry to the Senior Executive Service and are used by many executive-level departments and agencies in the selection, performance management, and leadership development for management and executive positions. The ECQs are used to select for all career SES positions and also guide the development of those already in Senior Executive Service positions.

As part of their succession planning, some agencies are beginning to look for the leadership skills required for executives earlier in the selection process—including using the ECQs in the selection of GS-14 and GS-15 level positions.

Executive qualifications are the primary selection criteria for the SES. While technical job-specific qualifications are important, the essence of the SES is the ability to lead. OPM has developed Executive Core Qualifications (ECQs) that represent the critical leadership skills all executives need to succeed today and in the future. OPM's policy is that ECQs should constitute at least 50%, and preferably more, of the weight when selecting for the SES.

The current ECQs are Leading Change; Leading People; Results Driven; Business Acumen; and Building Coalitions. These ECQs represent a shift from passive management to active leadership. The emphasis today is on innovation, vision, and programmatic shifts that result in organizational change and performance, rather than on managing a process.

Executive Core Qualifications (ECQs)

Leading Change	This core qualification involves the ability to bring about strategic change, both within and outside the organization, to meet organizational goals. Inherent to this ECQ is the ability to establish an organizational vision and to implement it in a continuously changing environment.
Leading People	This core qualification involves the ability to lead people toward meeting the organization's vision, mission, and goals. Inherent to this ECQ is the ability to provide an inclusive workplace that fosters the development of others, facilitates cooperation and teamwork, and supports constructive resolution of conflicts.
Results Driven	This core qualification involves the ability to meet organizational goals and customer expectations. Inherent to this ECQ is the ability to make decisions that produce high-quality results by applying technical knowledge, analyzing problems, and calculating risks.
Business Acumen	This core qualification involves the ability to manage human, financial, and information resources strategically.
Building Coalitions	This core qualification involves the ability to build coalitions internally and with other federal agencies, state and local governments, nonprofit and private sector organizations, foreign governments, or international organizations to achieve common goals.

Leadership and Fundamental Competencies

Competencies are the personal and professional attributes that are critical to successful performance in the SES. There are 28 competencies. Twenty-two of them are the specific competencies for the Executive Core Qualifications (ECQs), with each ECQ representing a "bundle" of related competencies from the 22. The remaining six are the fundamental competencies and together serve as the foundation for all of the ECQs.

A well-prepared ECQ statement reflects the underlying ECQ-specific competencies (e.g., "Leading Change" reflects creativity and innovation, external awareness, etc.). Because the fundamental competencies are cross-cutting, they should be addressed throughout the complete ECQ narrative. It is not necessary to address them directly as long as the narrative, in its totality, shows mastery of these fundamental competencies. Experience and training that strengthen and demonstrate the competencies will enhance a candidate's overall qualifications for the SES.

The Six Cross-Cutting Fundamental Competencies

Interpersonal Skills	Treats others with courtesy, sensitivity, and respect. Considers and responds appropriately to the needs and feelings of different people in different situations. {**Writers' Tip:** This competency can be easily addressed in Leading People and Building Coalitions stories by describing how you interact with other people.}
Oral Communication	Makes clear and convincing oral presentations. Listens effectively; clarifies information as needed. {**Writers' Tip:** This competency can be addressed in many ECQs—examples of conducting negotiations or briefing leadership validate oral communications.}
Integrity/Honesty	Behaves in an honest, fair, and ethical manner. Shows consistency in words and actions. Models high standards of ethics. {**Writers' Tip:** An example of integrity and honesty may be found in a story about conflict resolution or funds administration/financial stewardship.}
Written Communication	Writes in a clear, concise, organized, and convincing manner for the intended audience. {**Writers' Tip:** This competency can be described in a story about preparing high-level presentations and reports for use by Congress; legal briefs, meeting agendas, budget justifications, contracts, and/or books and peer-reviewed publications.}
Continual Learning	Assesses and recognizes own strengths and weaknesses; pursues self-development. {**Writers' Tip:** Continual Learning may be addressed in examples of higher education, attendance and participation at high-level symposia, or completion of an SES development program.}
Public Service Motivation	Shows a commitment to serve the public. Ensures that actions meet public needs; aligns organizational objectives and practices with public interests. {**Writers' Tip:** Public Service Motivation is expressed in continually serving customers—being on the forefront of developing and implementing programs to serve the public. It may also be expressed in supporting management and subordinates to create successful programs.}

The New Five-Page SES Federal Resume

In 2009, the U.S. Office of Personnel Management (OPM) began permitting agencies to recruit for and select new members of the SES based on an applicant's resume. The concept behind the new method is straightforward. It is intended to attract more highly qualified applicants for the SES—those whose resumes "speak for themselves"—by making the process less onerous and shifting more of the burden to the human resources staffs in the recruiting agencies. This new approach represented a significant departure from the standard method of application, which requires the submission of separate narrative statements addressing each of the five ECQs. (Often, the term "ECQs" is used to refer to the essays as well as to the Executive Core Qualifications themselves. To avoid confusion, the term "ECQ essay" or "ECQ narrative" is used as often as possible in this book.)

OPM made the decision to go ahead with the new method after piloting it with several agencies during 2008. Results from the pilot were generally positive. As anticipated, the number of applications received rose significantly, and those applying responded favorably to the streamlined requirements, with some even expressing a preference for the new process over what they had experienced in the private sector. Human resources staff in the pilot agencies were less happy with the extra burden placed on them, although some of this could be attributed to lack of familiarity and the inevitable "growing pains" of implementing a new approach.

Since the initial pilot, agency use of the resume-based method for SES applications has grown slowly, and as of this writing, the traditional method requiring applicants to write narrative statements on the ECQs continues to be the predominant mode of application for the SES. In 2010, the President's Management Council initiated a second pilot aimed at increasing the use of the resume-based method. This along with a similar initiative to eliminate the requirement for narratives addressing knowledge, skills and abilities (KSAs) for non-SES positions is likely to bring about greater use of the resume-based method across Government.

SES Five-Page Resume in USAJOBS Format

Page 1 of the Five-Page SES Federal Resume in USAJOBS, Emphasizing ECQ Accomplishments

THEODORE ROOSEVELT

WORK EXPERIENCE

United States of America   **Nov. 1904 - Present**

**White House,
Washington, DC**

**Salary: $42,000 USD Per Year
Hours per week: 40**

26th President of the United States

In 1904, I won the Presidency by a landslide. "I am no longer a political accident." I introduced new excitement and power to the Presidency by vigorously leading Congress and the American public toward new reforms and a strong foreign policy. As the Steward of the People, I performed the following leadership initiatives, among many others.

KEY LEADERSHIP INITIATIVES:

• Established the Antiquities Act of June 8, 1906. Proclaimed "historic landmarks, historic or prehistoric structures, and other objects of historic or scientific interest" in federal ownership as national monuments. Established conservation actions that helped to impact what would one day become the National Park Service (NPS), which was formally established on August 25, 1916.

• Negotiated disputes over Venezuela, the Dominican Republic, and Morocco. Led the negotiations on the adoption of the Drago Doctrine, which prevented the use of force in collecting foreign debts, an issue increasingly important as the U.S. became more involved with other countries.

• Signed legislation that established five national park units: Crater Lake, Oregon; Wind Cave, South Dakota; Sullys Hill, North Dakota (later designated a game preserve); Mesa Verde, Colorado; and Platt, Oklahoma (now part of the Chickasaw National Recreation Area). By the end of 1906, I had proclaimed four national monuments: Devil's Tower, Wyoming; El Morro, New Mexico; Montezuma Castle, Arizona; and the Petrified Forest, Arizona. I also protected a large portion of the Grand Canyon as a national monument in 1908. During my presidency, I signed into law a total of 18 national monuments.

• In 1905, formed the United States Forestry Service and appointed Gifford Pinchot as the first chief of this new agency. For the first time, lands were reserved for public use and huge irrigation projects were started. The forest reserves in the U.S. went from approximately 43 million acres to about 194 million acres.

The SES Recruitment and Review Process

Executive Resources Board

After initial screening by the human resources office to eliminate obviously unqualified applicants, SES applications are given a first hard look by a group of reviewers consisting of either the agency's SES Executive Resources Board (ERB) or, more typically, a panel of SES members acting on its behalf. The ERB rates and ranks the applicants and identifies the best-qualified candidates to move forward.

The ERB evaluates the SES candidates to determine:

1. whether the candidate meets the all five Executive Core Qualifications (ECQs) at a minimum level;
2. the extent to which the application shows evidence of the 28 leadership competencies that underlie the ECQS; and
3. how well the candidate meets the Technical Qualifications (TQs) specific to the position.

Additional Assessments

The agency may require additional assessments as part of the screening process. For example, structured interviews are becoming increasingly more common and are required by OPM when the application is resume-based. Additional screening may also include a writing sample, assessment test, reference check, or secondary interview. The executive to whom the selectee will report may also interview best-qualified candidates as determined by the panel and may make a recommendation to the full ERB. The ERB will deliberate on all of the information and send forward one or more candidates to the selecting official (usually the agency head) for a tentative selection, subject to certification by an OPM-led Qualifications Review Board.

Qualifications Review Board (QRB)

The critical last step in the SES selection process is certification by the QRB. This group— administered by the Office of Personnel Management—is a rotating panel of three volunteer Senior Executive Service members who assemble once or twice a week to review tentative selections to the SES. The QRB provides an independent peer review of SES candidates for their first appointment to the SES. An SES candidate cannot be appointed to the SES until the QRB certifies his or her executive qualifications. The QRB helps ensure that the agency's selection process was unbiased and that technical skills do not outweigh leadership expertise in the selection of new senior executives.

Ordinarily the QRB primarily focuses on reviewing the ECQs, but in the case of a resume-based selection it must rely on the candidate's resume and other information provided by the agency, such as notes from the candidate's structured interview.

If your application is forwarded to the QRB and evaluated, here are the possible outcomes:

- If the QRB sees in your certification package that you have the leadership capabilities for an SES position in government, you will receive a notice that you are certified. This occurs in the large majority of cases.

- This QRB certification will then result in your being hired into the position. The certification is good for life (assuming you complete successfully the one year probation period), even if you leave the federal government and then return. Also, once you occupy a career SES position, you may seek reassignment to other SES positions without formally competing.

- If your certification package is disapproved by the Board, the selecting agency will receive detailed information about what is missing or otherwise insufficient. If the rejection is based on review of your written ECQ narratives, you will be given approximately four to eight weeks to resubmit the ECQs. (Chapter 7, Lessons Learned from Disapproval Letters, contains tips for writing successful ECQ narratives—whether they are submissions or resubmissions.) Similarly, when a resume-based selection is initially disapproved, the agency may submit additional evidence in order to make the case for certification.

- Resubmissions are successful in most cases, but if your submission is disapproved again, the agency has several options, such as re-advertising the position, changing the classification, or submitting a request for a "developmental" SES appointment, which if successful means final certification would be contingent on your participating in training or other developmental activities. These options are at the agency's discretion.

The Structured Interview

A structured interview is one in which all candidates are asked the same questions by an interview panel in the same order and in more or less the same way. This type of interview aims to provide a framework from which candidates can be compared and scored as objectively as possible.

Structured interviews are becoming an important part of the SES application process, not only because OPM requires agencies to conduct structured interviews when using the resume-based selection process described above, but also because some of the federal agencies that still use the ECQ narrative application are also starting to incorporate a structured interview into their SES selection process. Regardless of the application method, today's SES job applicant needs to be prepared to describe his or her ECQs effectively in an interview setting.

Read the entire chapter on *The Structured Interview* beginning on page 135.

"Today federal managers are increasingly turning to the Behavioral-Based Structured Interview as the best practice strategy in order to make the best hiring decisions into the ranks of the Senior Executive Service (SES). The reason for this is simple. This process has been validated as providing selecting officials with the best predictive evidence the person selected will be successful on the job. That person can be you!

The Behavioral Based Structured Interview is founded on the premise recent past behavior is the best predictor of future performance in similar circumstances. A Behavioral Based Structured Interview consists of carefully planned, job-related questions that can be systematically scored to reliably identify highly qualified job candidates."
- Tim Cannon, Retired SES and Col., USMC

The CCAR Model: Challenge | Context | Action | Result

OPM's recommended format for writing the Executive Core Qualifications is called the CCAR (Challenge, Context, Action, and Result) Model. Full ECQ essays must be in the CCAR format in order to be approved. The shorter mini-leadership bullets used in the five-page resume-based format may also be written in a summarized CCAR format, using some or all of the CCAR elements.

The Executive Resources Staff, rating and selecting officials, and Qualifications Review Board (QRB) members will be seeking specific information that validates a leadership story describing your achievements. You may also want to include professional and volunteer experience, education, training, and awards that demonstrate your leadership skills in a particular Executive Core Qualification (ECQ).

Developing an ECQ is much like writing any other essay. It has a brief summary introduction (the Challenge), a body (the Context and Action), and a conclusion (the Result).

Challenge: What was the specific problem that needed resolution? What made the achievement challenging? What were the sub-challenges that you faced?

- The challenges should describe a large-scope, organizational-level issue, with agency-wide, government-wide, or national/international effects or impacts.

- It should require more than individual actions and result in organizational impact.

Context: Define the factors (people, institutions, procedures) that made the challenge one of executive caliber. (Include dates, job title, and company name or project—the who, what, where, why, and when of the situation.)

- It should include redefinition of goals, changes in conditions, and some requirements to encourage other people or organizations to comply with your vision.

- Be specific in terms of factors that made the challenge substantial: resources, people, laws, regulations, deadlines, and complexity.

Action: What did you do that made a difference? What actions did you take?

- Express your achievement in a team environment, but focus on your role within the team.

Result: What difference did it make? Qualify and quantify results. Use numbers, dollar amounts, percentages. Use ripple effect examples (what other organizations did it reach or influence?).

- How did the accomplishment transform organizational performance? Metrics and quantifiable results are one of the most important components of the ECQs.

Warm-Up Exercise: Accomplishment Freewriting

Use the space below to practice writing one of your significant leadership accomplishments in the CCAR format. You can also use an online KSA / CCAR builder on the Resume Place website; type in your accomplishment story and have it emailed to you for cutting and pasting. Go to http://www.resume-place.com/ksa_builder/template/.

ECQ Title:

Challenge

Context

Action

Result

Glossary

CCAR: CCAR is the Challenge, Context, Action, and Result storytelling model for describing accomplishments. This model is recommended by OPM for writing the ECQ narratives and is highly effective for framing brief accomplishment descriptions for the five-page resume-based application. The CCAR method can also be used very effectively in preparation for the structured, behavior-based interview.

Cover Letter: A cover letter or letter of interest may accompany a senior executive application package. The cover letter should describe the applicant's interest in the position, provide brief examples of how the candidate's experience is a good fit for the position, and highlight strong leadership qualifications essential to the open position. It should also include the announcement number, position title, and a list of attachments. The cover letter can be one to one and a half pages and could help the candidate to stand out. Check the vacancy announcement to make sure the cover letter does not count against the five-page resume limit.

Executive Core Qualifications (ECQs): The five leadership ECQs determined by the Office of Personnel Management are: Leading Change, Leading People, Results Driven, Business Acumen, and Building Coalitions. Candidates must demonstrate clearly the scope, quality, and level of responsibility sufficient to successfully perform the duties and responsibilities of an executive position.

Executive Federal Resume: The executive federal resume is used for applying to GS-15 and SES applications and is prepared in the federal resume format. This resume is, on average, three to five pages and must include relevant Work Experience (from the last 10 years), Education, Certification, Awards, Relevant Training, and accomplishments that demonstrate your leadership skills. The ECQs and TQs do not need to be covered in the traditional format executive federal resume.

Five-Page SES Federal Resume: This is a new, streamlined, comprehensive federal resume format for SES applications required to be in the resume-based format. This resume can be no more than five pages in length, must include the ECQs within the context of the resume, and should provide information about accomplishments and TQs. This resume also must include your relevant Work Experience (from the last 10 years), Education, Certification, Awards, Relevant Training, and accomplishments that demonstrate the ECQs and TQs.

MTQs/PTQs/MTCs: These are alternate names for Technical Qualifications (TQs): Mandatory Technical Qualifications, Professional Technical Qualifications, Mandatory Technical Competencies, or similar.

Senior Executive Service Candidate Development Program (SES CDP):
This intensive OPM-sponsored program is designed to train, develop, and certify individuals who exhibit outstanding executive potential for SES positions.

Technical Qualifications (TQs): TQs are the Technical Qualifications that agencies require of candidates, specific to the position and agency. TQs may be required in essay format or integrated into the five-page SES resume-based application. Candidates must demonstrate experience and skills sufficient to successfully perform the duties and responsibilities of a particular executive level position.

ECQ: Business Acumen
Audit Training for Improving Customer Services

"Introduced a training program for 600 auditors within the Audit Service to eliminate the time that program personnel spent educating auditors, to dismantle barriers, and to cultivate better relationships between the internal audit and acquisition communities. The auditing reform and additional training initiative enhanced the Audit Service's credibility within the acquisition communities, increased our client focus and responsiveness, and expanded our inventory of products and services to meet client needs; 90% percent of our acquisition audits are now addressing the Army's high risk areas."

Read the entire five-page SES resume and more ECQ Accomplishments in Keith Smith's case study starting on page 160.

Chapter Two

Are You SES Ready?

The Leadership Journey

Focusing Your Learning for Career and Organizational Success

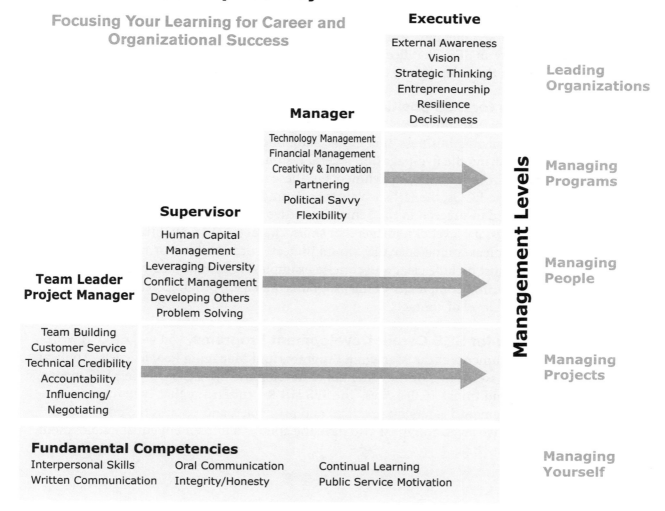

Executive
- External Awareness
- Vision
- Strategic Thinking
- Entrepreneurship
- Resilience
- Decisiveness

Manager
- Technology Management
- Financial Management
- Creativity & Innovation
- Partnering
- Political Savvy
- Flexibility

Supervisor
- Human Capital Management
- Leveraging Diversity
- Conflict Management
- Developing Others
- Problem Solving

**Team Leader
Project Manager**
- Team Building
- Customer Service
- Technical Credibility
- Accountability
- Influencing/Negotiating

Management Levels

- Leading Organizations
- Managing Programs
- Managing People
- Managing Projects
- Managing Yourself

Fundamental Competencies
Interpersonal Skills   Oral Communication   Continual Learning
Written Communication   Integrity/Honesty   Public Service Motivation

How Is Your Leadership Journey Going?

This Leadership Journey chart on the previous page was developed by the Office of Personnel Management. The chart is used to help individuals and agencies build the development segment of their Succession Plan. The graphic lays out the 28 OPM leadership competencies. The competencies serve as the roadmap for leadership development.

The core leadership competencies are basic competencies for all employees. Research indicates that without these core competencies, success at upper levels is not possible.

The graphic illustrates the customary levels of management and leadership. Associated with each level are related competencies that are critical for success at that level and form a developmental step for the next level of management or leadership. There are key experiences at each level that are designed to reinforce the associated competencies.

The major test of SES readiness is in the accomplishments that you will write for your ECQs. Are they at the Leading Organizations level? Are they at the Managing Programs level? The ECQs will determine if you are qualified today for an SES position, or qualified for an SES Candidate Development Program, in which you will participate in developmental assignments and executive leadership training for up to two years before you can submit your ECQs to OPM for certification as an SES member. Candidates who successfully complete the program and obtain certification by an SES Qualifications Review Board (QRB) may be selected for an SES position anywhere in the federal government without further competition.

In order to qualify for SES positions, your ECQ accomplishments should be at the Leading Organizations/Executive level, where you are leading change, leading people, achieving results, managing business operations, and building coalitions. The SES vacancy announcements requiring the five-page SES federal resume state: "It is highly recommended that your resume address your accomplishments in these specific competency areas." For the traditional 10-page ECQs, the HR specialists recommend: "The ECQs assess the broad executive skills needed to succeed in the Senior Executive Service (SES). The narrative should demonstrate the necessary level of management skills, characteristics, qualities, specialized knowledge, and technical competence that would indicate successful performance in the SES. This evidence must include clear and concise examples that emphasize your level of responsibilities, scope and complexity of the programs managed, program accomplishments, policy initiatives, and level of contacts."

In order to qualify for SES Career Development Programs, you will need to write your ECQ accomplishments at the Managing Programs and Managing People levels. Applicants must demonstrate possession of or the potential to develop the five ECQs in their SES five-page resume, or in their traditional ECQ essays. The SES HR Recruiters say that "you must have knowledge of management/leadership practices and principles, and possess the potential to function at an executive level. You must also have the ability to implement equal employment opportunity."

Accomplishment Examples

Do you have the level of accomplishments that will get you an SES position? It seems subtle, but the SES human resources recruiters know the difference between a manager who manages programs (and is therefore not SES ready) and an executive who leads organizations and is primed to be an SES candidate.

Read the examples of the following Accomplishment Samples and Federal Resume Accomplishments to see the differences between accomplishment levels: Leading Organizations, Managing Programs, and Managing Projects. The Leading Organizations examples are at the appropriate level for SES applications. The rest of the examples are excellent candidates for SES CDP applications.

Accomplishment Example #1: LEADING ORGANIZATIONS (SES Ready)

Leadership competencies demonstrated: *External Awareness, Vision, Strategic Thinking, Entrepreneurship, Resilience, Decisiveness - GS 14 and up*

Logistics Management Operations: As Deputy Support Operations Officer, HQ 13th Corps Support Command, Ft. Hood, TX, directly support Global War on Terrorism, preparing, planning, and managing logistical operations for 200,000 active-duty and reserve troops assigned to Ft. Hood and geographically separate 3rd Corps units. Evaluate and implement all aspects of logistics assistance mission activities. Integrate logistics including financial, transportation, road network planning, supply chain support, and material life cycle management. Develop logistics operations to support task force operations, equipment, and personnel. Ensure supplies and equipment are in place with troops and arrange for re-supply as needed. Coordinate with other military organizations and government agencies to secure goods.

Deployed for Joint Task Force Katrina, Hurricanes Katrina, Rita, 09-10/05
Deployed for Joint Task Force Katrina to provide mission support to relief efforts. Sent in 4 days after Hurricane Katrina to establish warehousing and distribution operations center for active-duty military. Grew assignment to support city of New Orleans to receive and distribute FEMA aid to local emergency workers and residents. Analyzed situation and developed action plan. Assumed distribution management: Established priorities and coordinated and moved supplies to distribution points. Worked directly with local officials to support recovery operations. Established system for logistical support—received water, life support, vehicles, etc., for 18,000 firefighters; federal, state, and local employees; and Army National Guard. After system was in place, turned over management to city officials and continued in advisory role. Throughout assignment, led staff of 15, logistically supporting 25,000 active-duty Army service members. Upon arrival of Rita, deployed to Lake Charles and Cameron Parish. At end of duty assignment, ensured situation had transitioned from crisis management to recovery planning and operations.

Project Implementation Manager on a wide range of complex DoD enterprise-wide information technology projects to include Defense Agencies Branch, Programs and Implementation Division. Directed project staffs in executing DISA IT program plans and objectives. Prepared, monitored and implemented project timelines using Microsoft Project software. Obtained equipment through acquisition process: employed cost justifications, submitted bids and acquired systems within budget limits. Exceeded customer and agency timeline expectations by completing many projects ahead of schedule. Consulted with DoD agencies and DISA internal/external clients to define and analyze functional requirements and translated into technical specifications on the client's Service Request Form (SRF).

Spearheaded a reengineering effort of the acquisition auditing process at six major Army Acquisition Commands within the Department of the Army (DA). Several studies on the oversight of the acquisition process had criticized internal auditors. Provided oversight guidance to 26 major program offices executing 119 acquisition programs. My efforts resulted in the acquisition reform initiative changing how the DA Acquisition community views the Army Audit Service. DA Senior Acquisition Leaders issued endorsement letters validating the success of this acquisition reform and their support for continuation. This acquisition reform initiative moved the Program Executive Office to the forefront of implementation of innovative programs.

Accomplishment Example #2: **MANAGING PROGRAMS (SES CDP Possible)**

Leadership competencies demonstrated: Technology Management, Financial Management, Creativity and Innovation, Partnering, Political Savvy, Flexibility - GS 13/14

Utilized Lean Six Sigma to create Service Request Form (SRF) Improvement
As Implementation Project Manager, I successfully completed customer's SRF and delivery to the Business Office to ultimately deliver a Letter Estimate (LE) to the customer that contained the customer solution, summary of requirements, estimated costs, project approach and timeline, and implementation plan. I developed a leaner, more time-efficient process oriented toward greater customer satisfaction. This initiative facilitated an improved service level management, ensuring that agreed services were delivered effectively and efficiently with maximum customer satisfaction.

Crafted deployment order and plans to move 13th COSCOM Operation to Iraqi theater from 45 separate locations. Executed logistical support plan for 600 troops. At completion of tour, handed over operations to new unit, coordinated return logistics, and reestablished operations in Ft. Hood. Spearheaded reintegration of Brigade forward and rear elements and jump-started home station training plans. Managed enrollment of unit equipment into reset or reconstitution programs to get them ready for future missions.

Project Manager for multiple projects in Iraq to support operations mission.
Managed aspects of project planning, execution and close-out of one or more projects. Utilized performance management and measurement methods, tools and techniques. Developed detailed project plans and schedules. Gathered and facilitated definition of project scope and requirements. Provided key advice to Iraqi counterparts during the fielding of 300+ combat vehicles, with a value in excess of $31 million. Resulted in increased protection of personnel and the saving of countless lives. Oversaw planning and construction of $15-million Iraqi Army Headquarters facility, resulting in increased personnel morale and unit efficiency. Supervised $3-million renovation of a US Army base camp. Positively impacted readiness and morale of the unit. Planned and supervised turn-in of 33 US vehicles with value in excess of $17 million, and fielding of 45 US vehicles with a value in excess of $50 million. Resulted in increased personnel protection and unit readiness.

Accomplishment Example #3: **MANAGING PEOPLE (SES CDP Possible)**

Leadership competencies demonstrated: *Human Capital Management, Leveraging Diversity, Conflict Management, Developing Others, Problem Solving - GS 12/13*

Supervised and provided management support on recruitment for 5 managers within a 5,000 person agency. Ensured requests completed and deadlines were met. Trained and mentored staff, delegated tasks. Analyzed and consulted on human resources issues with customers. Provided timely, accurate and professional responses in the areas of recruitment, placement, position management, pay administration, employee/labor relations, employee performance evaluations, individual development plans, disciplinary actions, incentive awards, employee services and benefits. Reviewed standard operating procedures, OPM regulations and multiple policy revisions to render recommendations and commentary on the impact of the agency's mission and goals.

Implemented revised program operations and automated recruitment systems. Participated in extensive reviews of revised program operations and new program projections in utilizing organizational development and workforce strategic planning. Methodologies consisted of major management objectives, program goals, priorities and current/anticipated workloads, and resource requirements.

- Advised on the redesign of the recruitment process to effectively implement new authorities and enhancements in program structures.
- Member of Assessment Development Team implementing USA Staffing recruitment system; department converted from QuickHire to USA Staffing system in November 2010.

Directed 45 military and civilian clerical, administrative and supply support personnel. Planned, prepared, and revised work schedules and duty assignments according to budget allotments, customer needs, employee capabilities, problems, and workloads. Verified completeness and accuracy of work. Monitored and effected changes for military and civilian manpower allocations, requirements and authorization for United States Military Entrance Processing Command. Planned, coordinated and scheduled the installation of a $76,000 dollar security system for a 27,000+ sf facility while Security Manager. Brought entire building into compliance with Anti-Terrorism guidelines for stand-alone Federal Buildings. Helped control access to the building for security purposes. Ensured that the facility met Inspector General's requirements. Improved process for staff checking in and out of the organization from seven days to one.

Accomplishment Example #4: MANAGING PROJECTS (SES CDP Possible)

Leadership competencies demonstrated: Team Building, Customer Service, Technical Credibility, Accountability, Influencing/Negotiating - GS 11/12

Led the project team for an SMS Upgrade. Tasked to upgrade from SMS 2.0 to SMS 2003 with minimal interruption to the production environment. Developed and executed a detailed project plan and led a 15-person technical team through the configuration, integration, pilot, and rapid deployment stages to upgrade 80 SMS servers providing enterprise management for more than 250 servers and 5,000 client workstations (2005).

Review, administer and close food aid agreements. Demonstrate knowledge of Federal Acquisition Regulations and contract laws to perform reviews of agreement language and Logistics and Monetization reports submitted by Private Voluntary Organizations for the Office of Capacity Building and Development food assistance programs including Food for Progress and Food for Education. Review budgets; compare reports to determine success of program.

My role is combating world hunger. As an Agricultural Marketing Specialist, I helped enable the USDA to implement a $2.9 million food processing agreement with Zambia. I read the agreement language, closed the deal, reviewed report logs and checked audits. I ensured proper shipping costs and fair prices. Despite logistical challenges and potential fraud, my awareness of details and procedures ensured that there were no major commodity losses.

- RESULT: The USDA food program successfully functioned in areas frequently plagued by hunger.

Manage administrative services for 88 military and civilian employees, including workforce planning, human resources, budget, training, facilities, records management, security and administrative support.

- Honored as Senior Civilian of the Quarter, October-December 2010, "for exceptional performance of duty while serving as Administrative Officer."

- Appointed as Approving/Certifying Official for Government Credit Purchase Card Program.

- Appointed as Authorizing Official for Defense Travel System.

System Administrator, Learning Management System (LMS) for local facility service and Regional duties. LMS Domain Manager; Service Training Coordinator for Information Technology Service. Monitored service staff member compliance with training requirements. Identified performance measures.

- Improved completion rate from 40 percent to 95 percent of all staff for VA mandatory annual training.

- Initiated use of Microsoft Live Meeting to share training dates, subject matter, and location. Used Live Meeting to conduct training for off-site employees.

- Initiated face-to-face contact with 100 percent of staff to inform of training requirements, follow up to see that training was conducted, and offer assistance to complete online training requirements.

- Instructed all staff on how to complete online National Mandated training; initiated use of Microsoft live to inform all staff members of training dates, subject matter and location.

Federal Resume Accomplishment Examples

Federal resumes also demonstrate your level of accomplishment along the Leadership Journey. In order to qualify for SES positions, you will need to write your federal resume with an emphasis on Leading Organizations. The following examples indicate the type and level of accomplishment.

Resume Example #1: **LEADING ORGANIZATIONS (SES Ready)**

DEPARTMENT OF DEFENSE, 1987 - PRESENT

Audit Director (YC-3 GS-0511 / GS-15 equivalent)   **11/2004 - Present**
Department of Army, Washington, DC   **Hours: 40/Week**
Supervisor: Sherri Jones; 555.202.3861 (may be contacted)

Oversee the activities of 1,000 professional auditors, to include Defense Contract Management Agency, Army Systems Command Earned Value Management Technical Experts, and Defense Contract Agency Audit auditors, divided among five audit teams; supervise a direct-report leadership staff and delegate authority for program execution. Pointed the way for major financial management control changes to the program and organizational elements, and financial management reviews of all DoD major acquisition programs. Report directly to the Assistant Auditor General of the Army for Research, Development, and Acquisition Audits.

Oversee strategic planning and execution of difficult and complex audits of multimillion-dollar Department of Army (DA) geographically dispersed weapon systems acquisition programs. Navigated through challenging agency and contractor resistance, and drove numerous organizational improvements, resulting in the establishment of an Earned Value Management (EVM) Integrated Process Team, EVM Center of Excellence, and EVM policy and procedures changes within the Department of the Army.

Leadership Accomplishments

- Routinely appointed as the Acting Assistant Auditor General for Research, Development, Acquisition, and Logistics Directorate, a Senior Executive Service (SES) level position, with executive management for 60 professional auditors. Brief the Secretary of the Army, the Under Secretary of the Army, the Assistant Secretary of Army for Research, Development and Acquisition, the Assistant Secretary of the Army for Financial Management and Comptroller and numerous Flag Officers, Secretariat-level, and other Senior Executives on financial management issues concerning a major defense acquisition programs.

- Transformed use of Earned Value Management (EVM) within DoD and Department of Army (DA). Led a large highly complex audit, requested by the Assistant Secretary of the Army, to determine what changes were needed to reinvigorate the EVM program and use it effectively across all DoD acquisition programs to achieve its strategic goal of providing affordable weapon systems to Sailors and Marines. Communicating my vision to reverse the problems and redirect the program, I guided Senior Acquisition leadership in assessing risks to improve efficiency, accountability, and program effectiveness. I then unveiled my audit strategy plan, and introduced a major shift in the method of conducting business with defense contractors; I led my teams into the offices of major defense contractors to evaluate the adequacy of their EVM systems against industry and DoD standards, a first-ever for the Army Audit Service. The results of my change initiative transformed use of EVM in DoD and with DoD contractors, ensuring program offices properly used EVM as a management tool and Soldiers and Sailors received affordable, timely weapon systems.

- Spurred the development and implementation of new DoD-wide policies and formed and led a high-level DoD working group composed of senior members from all DoD agencies to ascertain priority and proper use of EVM, establish and launch a Joint training program at the Defense Acquisition Contractor University, and create a DoD EVM Center to retrain the workforce and implement the policies to control costs for weapons development.

PROFILE: Logistics and operations professional with more than 20 years of expertise in all aspects of personnel and supply movement. Currently manage supply logistics program for active-duty and reserve troops in 3rd U.S. Corps. Excellent strategist and administrator, able to lead staff to achieve challenging short- and long-term goals. Superb communications skills, able to establish trust with internal staff and external customers, including other military branches, federal agencies, and state and local authorities; Joint Service Officer since 2006. Demonstrated crisis management skills, able to critically assess situation, options, and outcomes and make sound decisions. Skilled in developing and implementing policies and procedures and managing projects and programs.

PROFESSIONAL EXPERIENCE
      06/2006-present
      Deputy Support Operations Officer, Lieutenant Colonel
      HQ, 13th Corps Support Command, Ft. Hood, TX 76544

LOGISTICS MANAGEMENT OPERATIONS: Directly support Global War on Terrorism, preparing, planning, and managing logistical operations for 200,000 active-duty and reserve troops assigned to Ft. Hood and geographically separate 3rd Corps units. Evaluate and implement all aspects of logistics assistance mission activities. Integrate logistics including financial, transportation, road network planning, supply chain support, and material life cycle management. Develop logistics operations to support task force operations, equipment, and personnel. Ensure supplies and equipment are in place with troops and arrange for re-supply as needed. Coordinate with other military organizations and government agencies to secure goods.

DIRECT AND SUPERVISE logistics and administrative personnel, with 14 managers directly reporting. Train employees on technical regulations, policies, and procedures. Set priorities and assign tasks. Guide employees to resolve difficult technical issues and problems. Mentor and coach employees to ensure best performance and career satisfaction. Monitor and evaluate performance; implement/recommend corrective actions. Recognize staff performance in multitasking, deadline management, problem-solving, and teamwork.

PROGRAM MANAGEMENT: Develop reports and provide status information for US Army leadership use in operations planning and decision making.

SPECIAL ASSIGNMENTS

DISASTER / EMERGENCY MANAGEMENT: Hurricanes Katrina, Rita, 09-10/05

Deployed for Joint Task Force Katrina to provide mission support to relief efforts. Sent in 4 days after Hurricane Katrina to establish warehousing and distribution operations center for active-duty military. Grew assignment to support city of New Orleans to receive and distribute FEMA aid to local emergency workers and residents. Analyzed situation and developed action plan. Assumed distribution management: Established priorities and coordinated and moved supplies to distribution points. Worked directly with local officials to support recovery operations. Established system for logistical support--received water, life support, vehicles, etc., for 18,000 firefighters; federal, state, and local employees; and Army National Guard. Controlled supplies and synchronized distribution. Devised and implemented forward planning for short- and long-term recovery and most efficient use of funds and resources. After system was in place, turned over management to city officials and continued in advisory role. Throughout assignment, led staff of 15, logistically supporting 25,000 active-duty Army service members. Upon arrival of Rita, deployed to Lake Charles and Cameron Parish. At end of duty assignment, ensured situation had transitioned from crisis management to recovery planning and operations.

Resume Example #3: **MANAGING PROGRAMS (SES CDP Possible)**

WORK EXPERIENCE

US Department of Agriculture, Foreign Agriculture Service, Washington, DC
11/2004 - Present
Grade Level: GS-13
AGRICULTURAL MARKETING SPECIALIST, 1146

REVIEW, ADMINISTER AND CLOSE FOOD AID AGREEMENTS

Demonstrate knowledge of Federal Acquisition Regulations and contract laws to perform reviews of agreement language and Logistics and Monetization reports submitted by Private Voluntary Organizations for the Office of Capacity Building and Development food assistance programs including Food for Progress and Food for Education. Review budgets; compare reports to determine success of program.

• My role is combating world hunger. As an Agricultural Marketing Specialist, I helped enable the USDA to implement a $2.9 million food processing agreement with Zambia. I read the agreement language, closed the deal, reviewed report logs and checked audits. I ensured proper shipping costs and fair prices. Despite logistical challenges and potential fraud, my awareness of details and procedures ensured that there were no major commodity losses.

• RESULT: The USDA food program successfully functioned in areas frequently plagued by hunger.

ANALYZE POST-AWARD CONTRACTS FOR FOREIGN FOOD SERVICE

Review and analyze Reports of Independent Auditors on Internal Control over Financial Reporting, Compliance and other matters based on an audit of financial statements performed in accordance with Government Auditing Standards to determine if there were any reportable conditions. Determine and resolve cases where there are findings on Federal Award and Question Costs; report on status of the previous year's findings and resolution.

• I helped desperately poor people in the third world. I supervised multiple agreements that funded micro and mini entrepreneurs through FINCA (Foundation for International Community Assistance). I negotiated deals to help fund family farms that needed to boost agricultural production. Funds also went to HIV patients, including many women who were primary breadwinners and caring for infants.

ANALYZE ACQUISITION PLANS

Monitor and evaluate data to ensure that all objectives and criteria for measuring progress have been met including amounts sold, distributed, bartered, lost or destroyed, budget, audit, reporting and tax requirements, along with the results of the program. Provide success stories – written and pictures – to Public Affairs of unexpected outcomes for a program. The information is forwarded to Congress for a yearly report and snippets are posted on the FAS's website.

ANALYZE CONTRACT PRICE / COST DATA AND PROCUREMENT ACTIONS

As the lead for government-to-government food aid agreements, analyze data submitted by the governments of specific countries and Private Voluntary Organizations (PVO's) designated by the program. Review agreements for completeness and accuracy in keeping with the program's closure regulations. In addition, review tax certifications, lists of equipment valued at more than $5,000 purchased in host countries, and how assets will be disposed.

DEPARTMENT OF HEALTH AND HUMAN SERVICES
HUMAN RESOURCES SPECIALIST (GS-201-12)   Oct. 2007 to Present
Food & Drug Administration (FDA), Center for Food Safety and Applied Nutrition
Washington DC 20350
Hours per Week: 40, Salary per year: $ 82,359

PROVIDE HIGH QUALITY FEDERAL STAFFING AND CLASSIFICATION SERVICES. As senior Human Resources Specialist manage day-to-day human resource operations within the Recruitment, Hiring and Staffing Center. Expert in merit employment, pay demonstration, delegating examining, student employment and researching internal policies in accordance with OPM and HHS compliance.

IMPLEMENTED REVISED PROGRAM OPERATIONS AND AUTOMATED RECRUITMENT SYSTEMS. Participated in extensive reviews of revised program operations and new program projections in utilizing organizational development and workforce strategic planning. Methodologies consisted of major management objectives, program goals, priorities and current/anticipated workloads, and resource requirements.

• Advised on the redesign of the recruitment process to effectively implement new authorities and enhancements in program structures.

• Member of Assessment Development Team implementing USA Staffing recruitment system; department converted from QuickHire to USA Staffing system in November 2010.

SUPERVISED AND PROVIDED MANAGER SUPPORT on recruitment for 5 managers within a 5,000 person agency. Ensured requests completed and deadlines were met. Trained and mentored staff, delegated tasks.

ANALYZE AND CONSULT ON HUMAN RESOURCES ISSUES WITH CUSTOMERS. Provide timely, accurate and professional responses in the areas of recruitment, placement, position management, pay administration, employee/labor relations, employee performance evaluations, individual development plans, disciplinary actions, incentive awards, employee services and benefits.

DEMONSTRATED KNOWLEDGE OF RECRUITMENT, SELECTION AND PLACEMENT; developed crediting plans and job analysis through collaboration with managers and field personnel under Title 5, Title 38, Title 42, and special hiring authorities. Received applications for manual cases and conducted evaluation of applicant's eligibility through ranking and rating to prepare selection certificate based on qualifications, experience and education. Subsequent to selection of candidates, made job offer to applicants, established salaries and entered on-duty dates.

ADEPT IN UTILIZING RECRUITMENT AUTOMATION AND INFORMATION SYSTEMS; serve as super user and resident expert in the function of automated human resource systems such as QuickHire for recruitment and staffing, and QuickClass for position classification of positions. Comprehensive working knowledge of automated HR systems enhancements such as EWITS, PAWS, E-OPF's, RHRC Work log and IMPACT. Employed E-Induction program to prepare job offer letters, advise applicants of orientation process, reporting date and website link for completion of employment forms.

• Expert in staffing; identified as a QuickHire Super-user.

• Served on the assessment development team for USA Staffing.

WORK EXPERIENCE

Regional Legal Service Office   11/2009 - Present
Portland, OR US   Grade Level: 11
Salary: 68,000 USD Per Year

ADMINISTRATIVE OFFICER, 0341

MANAGE ADMINISTRATIVE SERVICES for 88 military and civilian employees, including workforce planning, human resources, budget, training, facilities, records management, security and administrative support.

• Honored as Senior Civilian of the Quarter, October-December 2010, "for exceptional performance of duty while serving as Administrative Officer."

• Appointed as Approving/Certifying Official for Government Credit Purchase Card Program.

• Appointed as Authorizing Official for Defense Travel System.

BUDGET MANAGER. Plan, develop, execute and monitor $1.5 million budget. Monitor and track budget execution, ensure all expenditures are consistent with plan; identify and resolve discrepancies.

• Received Time-Off & Performance Award, "for diligent dedication" in ensuring seamless systems integration and execution, for proper accounting and obligation of all FY-2010 budget dollars, and for improving working environments in offices throughout the region.

SUPERVISOR. Train, manage and supervise 7 civilian and military subordinates. Mentor them to exceed expectations and meet organizational goals; assign and monitor work; exercise full personnel authority including hiring, training, leave approval and discipline. Analyze and evaluate workforce needs. Make recommendations for increase and reallocation of staff, consistent with organizational goals.

FACILITIES MANAGER. Oversee and manage facilities consisting of 52,000 sf historic facility and grounds, including condition, rehabilitation and all related services. Manage upgrades, energy use and efficiency, safety and security, consistent with master plan, community design, and environmental standards.

• Oversaw and completed $4.1 million renovation of facilities on time.

WRITER AND EDITOR. Prepare written narrative and financial reports, analyses, policies, procedures and recommendations used by senior management for decision making. Use the full range of MS Office, including Word, Excel, PowerPoint and Outlook.

Exercise: Leadership Journey Assessment

Write one CCAR Accomplishment for your highest leadership level. You will have the opportunity to refine your accomplishment and write others in later chapters.

Which management level does your accomplishment best support? (check one)

- ☐ Leading Organizations – Executive
- ☐ Managing Programs – Manager
- ☐ Managing People – Supervisor
- ☐ Managing Projects – Team Leader / Project Leader
- ☐ Managing Yourself – Continual Learning / Education

Challenge:

_____
_____
_____
_____

Context:

_____
_____
_____

Action:

_____
_____
_____

Result:

_____
_____
_____
_____

ECQ: Leading Change
CIO, Delta Air Lines Enterprise Technology Turnaround Story

"As the CIO for Delta Air Lines, spearheaded the design of a long-term strategy / operational plan that would stretch corporate view to a three-year horizon by addressing short- and long-term planning, effectively forecasting all expenditures, and creating value for stakeholders. Winning approval from executive councils, the new planning process was embraced as a critical element of the Company's planning regimen. Capital spending dropped by 25% allowing for an increase in the capital spending program, reaching $1.5B."

Read the one-page CCAR version of this Leading Change ECQ starting on page 83.

Chapter Three

Different SES Application Formats

The Office of Personnel Management (OPM) conducted a pilot of innovative methods for SES selection in 2008. As a result, federal agencies now have a choice of using one of three processes for filling SES positions: the traditional format, the resume-based format, and the accomplishment record.

Each federal agency determines which application process to use, and each federal vacancy announcement posted for SES positions or SES CDP will specifically indicate which format is required by that agency for the posted position. Not only are there three different general formats available for agencies to choose from, agencies are not required to follow the standard OPM template for each of these formats and will often modify them or even create hybrid methods. Therefore, it is critical to read each vacancy announcement thoroughly, before applying for positions. Applicants may now be required to create two or three types of SES application packages with the associated required documents.

No matter which format is being used, the focus is still on the 28 Leadership Competencies identified by OPM. The QRB is seeking demonstrated and strong executive experience for initial career SES appointments. Candidates are selected for SES based on demonstrated evidence of executive experience as shown in the SES resume, ECQs (in any of the three identified formats), and structured interview.

Obviously, this diversity of application methods translates into a challenge for the applicant.

Our recommendation is to prepare the longest application format first—the traditional format—and be prepared to edit it down for the other variations.

In this book we will only address how to write the traditional and resume-based formats, but with the techniques and tips we provide, you will be prepared to address any of the application formats or requirements that you may encounter.

Three Most Common SES Application Formats

Traditional

The traditional SES application format is the lengthiest of the three described here—easily reaching 20 pages for a complete application package.

- Executive Federal Resume—three to five pages (including all the required federal elements, i.e., vacancy number, name, address, phone, email, job titles, dates, hours worked, salary, duties, accomplishments, education with dates, additional information)
- TQs—one page maximum for each
- ECQs—two examples or stories for each ECQ in the CCAR format, up to 8,000 characters each or 10 pages maximum, drawing from recent experience during the past 10 years
  - o Leading Change
  - o Leading People
  - o Results Driven
  - o Business Acumen
  - o Building Coalitions
- Cover Letter

Resume-Based (new)

This format and the next, the accomplishment record, were designed to be more streamlined and less burdensome than the traditional SES application format. The resume-based option was designed especially for high-level executive positions with difficult-to-meet requirements that would limit the number of applicants.

- Five-Page SES Federal Resume (with ECQs and TQs integrated within the context of the resume)
- Cover Letter

Accomplishment Record (new)

This method requires applicants to submit a resume and a shorter set of narratives addressing specific competencies (usually one from each ECQ). The essays are usually limited to one page each.

- Executive Federal Resume
- Selected Competencies—limited to one page for each
- Cover Letter

Sample Announcements

To show you how the application requirements look in some of today's vacancy announcements, we have listed below actual vacancy announcement language for a handful of current application formats. The application requirements are described in the Qualifications and How to Apply sections of the vacancy announcement. Be sure to read the instructions CAREFULLY and give yourself ample time (at least two days) to follow all of the directions and complete the application correctly.

The following samples include announcements for:

- Traditional Format (Resume plus 8-10 pages of ECQ Essays)
- Traditional Format with Questionnaire
- Five-Page SES Federal Resume Format
- Five-Page SES Federal Resume Format with Questionnaire
- Accomplishment Record
- SES CDP

If you are unsure about the application instructions, call or write the point of contact listed in the announcement.

Don't wait until the last minute to write and ask questions about the application. Think ahead and give yourself plenty of time.

Vacancy announcement language that applies to ALL applications:

"NOTE: THERE ARE UNIQUE APPLICATION INSTRUCTIONS FOR THIS VACANCY ANNOUNCEMENT. PLEASE READ APPLICATION INSTRUCTIONS CAREFULLY.

ALL APPLICANTS MUST SUBMIT THE FOLLOWING MATERIALS BY THE CLOSING DATE OF THE ANNOUNCEMENT. ONLY SUBMIT THE MATERIALS REQUESTED BY THIS ANNOUNCEMENT. APPLICATIONS RECEIVED AFTER THE CLOSING DATE OF THE ANNOUNCEMENT WILL NOT BE CONSIDERED."

Format #1 Traditional Format (8 to 10 pages)

The best way to identify whether a vacancy announcement is requesting the traditional format application is the length of the ECQ essays, which will be specified to be 8 to 10 pages. See the highlighted page lengths below.

Sample 1: Patent and Trademark Office

> **HOW TO APPLY:**
> Please be sure to include the following in your application packet: a resume, narratives describing your experience (specific tasks) and accomplishments against the four Professional Technical Qualifications (PTQs) and a SF-50. Please limit your PTQ narratives to no more than 2 pages per PTQ (8 pages total). Submit only the documents requested. Additional documents will not be reviewed by the rating panel. Please do not bind, tab, or place your application in a notebook.

Sample 2: US Department of Agriculture

> **MANDATORY QUALIFICATIONS**
> (Fully describe your qualifications for each Executive Core Qualification and Technical Qualification statements as an attachment with your application package).
>
> Applicants are encouraged to contact Deborah Crump at 301-504-1448, SeniorPositions@ars.usda.gov to obtain information on preparing your application package for this position in the Senior Executive Service.
>
> **HOW TO APPLY:**
> You must submit your application so that it will be received by the closing date of the announcement.
>
> 1. OF-612, Application for Federal Employment, OR resume that includes all specific information that your application must contain except your social security number (see 'Applying for a Federal Job: and forms at www.opm.gov./forms/html/of.asp)
>
> 2. Complete responses to executive and technical qualifications. (Managerial statements, i.e., ECQ's must not exceed 10 pages). Visit www.opm.gov./ses/recruitment/qualify.asp for additional guidance on writing your Qualifications Statements.

Sample 3: Department of Homeland Security, Federal Emergency Management Administration

1. Use one of the following: a resume; or Optional Application for Federal Employment Form (OF-612); or Application for Federal Employment (SF-171); or any other type-written format. Whichever version is used must include the following:

2. Narrative statement that addresses each Technical Qualification (no more than 4 pages total).

3. Narrative statement that addresses each Executive Core Qualification (ECQ) (no more than 10 pages total).

Sample 4: Department of Energy

QUALIFICATIONS REQUIRED:

To meet the minimum qualification requirements for this position, you must show that you possess the five Executive Core Qualifications (ECQs), Technical Qualifications, and other qualifications, if applicable.

Applicants for an initial SES career appointment must clearly demonstrate that they possess the broad executive core qualifications needed to succeed in the SES. The Office of Personnel Management (OPM) is required by law to review the executive qualifications of each new career appointee to the Senior Executive Service (SES) prior to appointment. To be considered for this position, applicants MUST submit a written statement addressing the Executive Core Qualifications (ECQs) listed below.

Current/former SES Career appointees and certified graduates of an OPM approved SES Candidate Development Program are not required to submit ECQ statements. All other applicants MUST address the ECQ's to be eligible for consideration. Your ECQ statements MUST NOT EXCEED 10 PAGES (if you exceed the maximum pages allowed, the system will be unable to process your application) and should focus on accomplishments that demonstrate each ECQ.

Format #2 Traditional Format (8 to 10 pages) with Questionnaire

Sample 1: HHS, OHR Executive Resources

Minimum Qualifications:

To meet the minimum qualification requirements for this position, you must respond to the assessment questionnaire for the mandatory technical qualifications and submit a resume, which provides evidence of how you possess the five ECQs.

Technical Qualifications:

All applicants must respond to the assessment questionnaire addressing the mandatory technical qualifications for this position. Click the following link to view and print the assessment questionnaire: View Occupational Questionnaire.

Executive Core Qualifications:

You will be prompted to provide narrative descriptions including specific examples of your experience, education, and accomplishments that are applicable to each of the following factors. Applicants are encouraged to visit http://www.opm.gov/ses/handbook.html and view the Office of Personnel Management's "Guide to Senior Executive Qualifications." Please use the Challenge, Context, Action, Results (CCAR) format that is suggested in the OPM guidance. Please review these qualifications and then follow the instructions found in the "How to Apply" section of this vacancy announcement. You will not be considered if you do not follow the instructions. Responses to the ECQs must not exceed 10 pages.

How to Apply:

To begin the process, click the Apply Online button to create an account or log in to your existing USAJOBS account. Follow the prompts to complete the assessment questionnaire. Please ensure you click the Submit My Answers button at the end of the process.

Note: To return to a previously Saved or Incomplete application you may use the following link: https://applicationmanager.gov/.

Applications for this vacancy MUST be received on-line via the USA Staffing web site before midnight Eastern Standard Time on the closing date of this announcement.

Sample 2: Department of Energy

HOW TO APPLY:

1.) Submit an online resume and respond to the job specific questions. Apply online at USAJOBS.

2.) If you are unable to apply online, call the Human Resources Specialist listed in the announcement between the hours of 8:00 a.m. to 5:00 p.m. Eastern Standard Time (EST).

3.) Submit all required documents by 11:59p.m. EST on the closing date of the announcement in order to receive consideration.

The Office of Personnel Management (OPM) is required by law to review the executive core qualifications of each new career appointee to the Senior Executive Service (SES) prior to appointment.

You must meet the technical and managerial qualification factors identified below. Failure by non-Senior Executive Service members to address each of the required Executive Core Qualifications (ECQ's) and Mandatory Technical Qualifications (MTQ's) statements will result in disqualification of your application. Your application must demonstrate that you possess these qualifications. Please, provide examples that are clear, concise, and emphasize your level of responsibilities, the scope and complexity of programs managed, program accomplishments, policy initiatives undertaken, and level of contacts. All qualified candidates will be evaluated on the relevance of their experience, education, training, self-development, honors, awards, and outside activities. Career Senior Executive Service Members who apply are expected to address only the MTQ's.

REQUIRED DOCUMENTS:

1. SUBMIT YOUR COMPLETED APPLICATION WHICH INCLUDES YOUR RESUME, YOUR RESPONSES TO ALL ONLINE ASSESSMENT QUESTIONS, and all required supplemental documents in order to be considered.

2. The documentation identified above must be attached to your application using one of the following actions:

1) "Upload" to upload documents directly from your computer

2) "USAJOBS" to upload documents stored in your "USAJOBS" accounts

3) "Fax" to generate a fax cover sheet and fax the documents (system generated cover sheet must be used)

Applicants will be prompted at the "Vacancy Documents" section of the application to add their required documents. Please review and follow the instructions listed to successfully submit your documents.

All Grades Questions

* 1. Are you currently serving or have served in the last five (5)years in a Political Appointment in the Federal Government?

○ Yes

○ No

* 2. I understand that the responses provided in this questionnaire must be fully supported in my online resume. I further understand that my resume must provide detailed descriptions and/or examples of my knowledge, skill, and abilities as required in the vacancy announcement and that my failure to do so, may result in my being rated "Ineligible" or "Not Qualified" for this position.

○ Yes

○ No

* 3. I understand as a Career Senior Executive Service Members I am required to address only the Mandatory Technical Qualifications (MTQs) and provide a copy of my Standard Form (SF-50) which shows proof of SES Status.

○ Yes

○ No

○ Not Applicable (I'm not a Career SES)

* 4. I understand as a non-Senior Executive Services (SES)Member; failure to address each of the required Executive Core Qualifications (ECQs) and Mandatory Technical Qualifications (MTQ's) statements will result in disqualification of my application.

○ Yes

○ No

○ Not Applicable (I'm a Career SES)

* 5. ECQ 1: Leading Change...... Please describe your Ability to bring about strategic change, both within and outside the organization, to meet organizational goals and to establish an organizational vision and to implement it in a continuously changing environment. (There is an 8000 word character limit. If you need additional space to complete your answer to this ECQ, you may add information in a follow-up question.)
Enter NA if Not Applicable.

(8000 character limit)

* 6. ECQ 2: Leading People...... Please describe your ability to lead people toward meeting the organization's vision, mission, and goals and to provide an inclusive workplace that fosters the development of others, facilitates cooperation and teamwork, and supports constructive resolution of conflicts. (There is an 8000 word character limit. If you need additional space to complete your answer to this ECQ, you may add information in a follow-up question.)
Enter NA if Not Applicable.

(8000 character limit)

* 7. ECQ 3: Results Driven...... Please describe your ability to meet organizational goals and customer expectations and to make decisions that produce high-quality results by applying technical knowledge, analyzing problems, and calculating risks. (There is an 8000 word character limit. If you need additional space to complete your answer to this ECQ, you may add information in a follow-up question.)
Enter NA if Not Applicable.

(8000 character limit)

Application Manager questions for sample on previous page

8000 characters is equivalent to about two pages. This announcement allows 8000 characters per ECQ essay, or 10 pages total for ECQs.

Format #3 Five-Page SES Federal Resume Format

Sample: Federal Aviation Administration

HOW TO APPLY:

Submit a current resume which describes your qualifications. Your resume must not exceed five pages including an optional cover letter. Information beyond five pages will not be evaluated.

Applications may be submitted electronically via email to Phyllis.Soldo@dot.gov or via fax at (202) 366-7890 and must be received by 11:59 pm Eastern Standard Time on the announcement closing date. If you have questions, call Phyllis Soldo at (202) 366-6376 or Arlene DiRienzo at (202) 366-2445.

Format #4 Five-Page SES Federal Resume Format with Questionnaire

Sample: Veterans Administration

REQUIRED DOCUMENTS:

A complete application for this position includes the following items:

1. Resume which demonstrates your experience, accomplishment, training, education and awards reflecting your ability to meet each of the MANDATORY executive core qualification requirement(s) for this position. Elaborate on your experience and accomplishments, highlighting your level of responsibilities, scope and complexity of programs managed, work objectives met (the results of your efforts), policy initiatives and level of contacts. Ensure your resume does not exceed five (5) pages. Information beyond the five page resume will not be evaluated. DO NOT submit the application form OF-612, Optional Application for Federal Employment in lieu of a resume. DO NOT submit separate narrative responses to address the executive core qualifications.

2. Complete responses to the Online Questionnaire. View Occupational Questionnaire

HOW TO APPLY:

We strongly encourage you to apply online. To begin, click the Apply Online button and follow the prompts to register and submit all required documents. To return to your saved application, login in to your USAJOBS account at http://www.usajobs.opm.gov/ and click on "Application Status". Click on the position title, and then select Apply Online to continue.

Format #5 Accomplishment Record

Sample: Department of Justice

Key Requirements:

- You must complete your resume and accomplishment record

- You must meet all minimum qualifications to be considered eligible

- JMD/HR must receive your application by 5:00 p.m. (EST) on the closing date

Qualifications:

To meet the minimum qualification requirements for this position, you must show that you possess the five Executive Core Qualifications (ECQs), Technical Qualifications, and other qualifications, if applicable, listed below.

EXECUTIVE CORE QUALIFICATIONS:

ECQ 1 - LEADING CHANGE: The ability to bring about strategic change, both within and outside the organization, to meet organizational goals. Inherent to this ECQ is the ability to establish an organizational vision and to implement it in a continuously changing environment.

ECQ 2 - LEADING PEOPLE: The ability to lead people toward meeting the organization's vision, mission, and goals. Inherent to this ECQ is the ability to provide an inclusive workplace that fosters the development of others, facilitates cooperation and teamwork, and supports constructive resolution of conflicts.

ECQ 3 - RESULTS DRIVEN: The ability to meet organizational goals and customer expectations. Inherent to this ECQ is the ability to make decisions that produce high-quality results by applying technical knowledge, analyzing problems, and calculating risks.

ECQ 4 - BUSINESS ACUMEN: The ability to manage human, financial, and information resources strategically.

ECQ 5 - BUILDING COALITIONS: The ability to build coalitions internally and with other Federal agencies, State and local governments, nonprofit and private sector organizations, foreign governments, or international organizations to achieve common goals.

Additional information on the ECQs is available at www.opm.gov/ses/recruitment/ecq.asp. Please do not submit narrative statements for each ECQ.

All applicants must submit written statements describing accomplishments that reflect your capability in five competencies related to the ECQs. You may submit one or two accomplishments for each competency. If you provide more than two accomplishments for a competency, only the first two accomplishments listed will be evaluated. Your response for each competency cannot exceed one page. The five competencies are:

1. Strategic Thinking - Formulates objectives and priorities, and implements plans consistent with the long-term interests of the organization in a global environment. Capitalizes on opportunities and manages risks.

2. Team Building- Inspires and fosters team commitment, spirit, pride, and trust. Facilitates cooperation and motivates team members to accomplish group goals.

3. Accountability - Holds self and others accountable for measurable high-quality, timely, and cost-effective results. Determines objectives, sets priorities, and delegates work. Accepts responsibility for mistakes. Complies with established control systems and rules.

4. Human Capital Management - Builds and manages workforce based on organizational goals, budget considerations, and staffing needs. Ensures that employees are appropriately recruited, selected, appraised, and rewarded; takes action to address performance problems. Manages a multi-sector workforce and a variety of work situations.

5. Influencing/Negotiating - Persuades others; builds consensus through give and take; gains cooperation from others.

For each accomplishment, you must include the following information: 1) a general statement of the situation or circumstances; 2) a precise description of exactly what activities you performed and the outcomes achieved; and 3) the start and end dates of the time period during which the activities were performed. You are required to respond to all competencies. Failure to do so will result in an incomplete accomplishment record and you will be rated as 'ineligible.' Additional instructions and an example accomplishment are available at www.opm.gov/ses/arinstructions.asp. You are strongly encouraged to review these additional instructions prior to preparing your narratives. Please note that highly qualified candidates will be asked to provide references who can verify the information provided.

Format #5 SES CDP

Job Title: Senior Executive Service Candidate Development Program
Agency: Social Security Administration
Salary Range: $123,758.00 - $155,500.00 /year
Series & Grade: GS-0301-15
Position Information: Full Time Temporary NTE 2 years

MAJOR DUTIES:
Program Overview:
SSA's SES CDP focuses on developing high-potential individuals who have demonstrated they have the ability to lead in a large complex organization. During their 18-24 month program, candidates must complete the following activities for successful completion of the program:

Competency Assessment: Candidates will complete a 360° assessment tool. Feedback from this will be used to identify developmental activities during the program that will strengthen or develop the leadership competencies and Executive Core Qualifications (ECQ).

Mentor Selection/Role: Each Candidate must select an SSA SES executive as a mentor from a list of ERB-approved mentor volunteers. Mentors must be from outside the Candidate's Deputy Commissioner-level component. The mentor will: assist in the development of the IDP; provide general guidance and advice throughout the program; provide regular reports to the ERB on Candidate progress; and concur or nonconcur in a Candidate's certification request at the end of the program.

Individual Development Plan: Selectees complete an Individual Development Plan (IDP which tracks with the five ECQs: Leading Change, Leading People, Results Driven, Business Acumen and Building Coalitions. The IDP is a fluid roadmap of developmental activities that address the Candidate's individual development needs and reinforces the concept of an "SES Corporate Culture." Prior to implementation, the IDP must be approved by the Candidate's mentor and SSA's ERB.

Developmental Assignments: Each Candidate must complete at least two developmental assignments during the program. All assignments must be consecutive and encompass the Candidate's 18-24 month program. Assignments must include exposure to SES-level activities and responsibilities.

* Two assignments must be a minimum of 6-months in length.
* Two assignments must be outside the Candidate's home component (Associate/Regional Commissioner) in a new occupational field. One of these must be outside the Candidate's Deputy-Commissioner-level component.
* One assignment must be external to SSA for at least 4 months. NOTE: Non-SSA selectees must complete all assignments at SSA.
* Headquarters Candidates must complete an assignment outside the Baltimore/Washington commuting area in a claims-related/hearing component (SSA Regional Office, Area Director Office, Program Service Center, Teleservice Center, or Hearing Office).
* Candidates from field offices must complete a staff assignment at SSA Headquarters (Baltimore/Washington commuting area).

Training: Candidates must attend the SES CDP Orientation and all Core training Programs. They must also complete 80 hours of executive-level interagency training related to the ECQs.

Other Learning Activities:
* Candidates must complete two executive interviews with an SES executive outside of their home component or executives outside of SSA.
* Candidates must complete a 1-day shadow assignment with an SES executive who is not his/her mentor.
* Candidates must read at least two books related to the ECQs.

QUALIFICATIONS: What are the minimum qualifications?

Executive Core Qualifications

Applicants must demonstrate possession of or the potential to develop in the five ECQs (described below). We recommend that your resume emphasize the level of your responsibilities, the scope and complexity of programs and offices managed, and program accomplishments.

Technical Qualifications

Applicants must have 52 weeks of experience at the GS-14 level or above (or equivalent) planning, managing or administering insurance program(s) that provide protection against socially recognized conditions, including poverty, old-age, disability, unemployment, and/or health in either the public or private sector.

HOW YOU WILL BE EVALUATED:

All applicants will be evaluated against the same criteria; i.e. the degree to which they demonstrate the potential to perform in a senior executive position. Applications will be screened to ensure applicants meet the basic qualifications for the program. The following tools will be used to evaluate applicants:

Step 1: Applicant's Executive Qualifications (AEQ) Questionnaire Maximum 50 Points
View Occupational Questionnaire

Step 2: Written Narratives Maximum 50 Points

Applicants in the Highly Qualified category will be invited to complete narrative statements supporting your selected proficiency levels. Please note that there will be a limited time to respond. Failure to complete these narrative statements by the deadline will remove you from consideration.

Step 3: Assessment Center Maximum 200 Points

Highly Qualified applicants will participate in a full-day assessment center in the Baltimore metropolitan area. Candidates will be evaluated by teams of SES executives in a variety of exercises to measure the applicant's potential in the five ECQs. Applicants who successfully complete the preceding evaluation will be referred for selection consideration.

Step 4: Executive Resources Board Review

The ERB may interview some or all of the Highly Qualified applicants and will make recommendations for selection to the Agency Head. The Agency Head makes the final selections for the program. Selectees will be notified through their home offices or directly, if they are external applicants. Applicants who are not selected will also be notified and provided their scores after selections have been announced.

Your application will be evaluated under the Category Rating method, based on your responses to the Assessment Questions. If you meet the basic requirements for the position, your application will be evaluated and placed into one of three categories:

1 - Qualified Category - Candidates who meet the Minimum Qualification Requirements.
2 - Well Qualified Category - Candidates who meet the Minimum Qualification Requirements and demonstrate a satisfactory level of the knowledge, skills, and abilities necessary to perform the duties of the position.
3 - Best Qualified Category - Candidates who meet the Minimum Qualification Requirements and demonstrate a high level of the knowledge, skills, and abilities necessary to perform the duties of the position.

Candidates eligible for veterans' preference will be placed ahead of other candidates in the appropriate category for which they have been rated. Additionally, preference eligibles who have a compensable service-connected disability of at least 10 percent and who meet the Minimum Qualification Requirements will automatically be placed in the Best Qualified Category.

Agency-Specific Requirements

Many agencies hire senior executive level and senior professional or SES-equivalent candidates using application requirements specific to the agency. SES candidates' ECQs are certified by a Qualifications Review Board, according to OPM's requirements. Some excepted agencies and non-career SES positions may have different application requirements, which do not require approval through OPM or a QRB.

The bottom line is, if you prepare a full traditional version of an SES package with an executive federal resume, a full set of ECQ essays, and several TQ essays, you will be very prepared to draw from this portfolio of documents to respond to vacancy announcements from different agencies that post varied applications requirements, as the executive or senior level requirements and competencies for those requirements are often similar to ECQs. The more accomplishment stories you develop, the larger your library of stories to draw from in order to complete varied application packages. Moreover, the added benefit of preparing a full executive resume and ECQ package is that you will also be drafting content for the structured/behavior-based interview.

To help you prepare for varied announcement requirements, here is a short list of some of the different requirements you may encounter from various agencies when applying for SES, senior level, GS-15, or SES-equivalent positions. These requirements may be in addition to a resume, ECQs, cover letter, or other requirements. Application requirements may also vary within the same agency, so always be sure to review the application requirements thoroughly before applying for a position.

The **Federal Aviation Administration (FAA)** uses the FAA Executive System (FAES): http://www.faa.gov/about/office_org/headquarters_offices/ahr/jobs_careers/exec_opportunities/exec_vacancies/how/. The FAA requests its executive applicants to complete Dimensions: 1. Achieving Operational Results; 2. Leading People; 3. Building Relationships; 4. Leading Strategic Change. These are separate essays in addition to the resume.

The **Intelligence Community (IC)** now requires Senior Executive Officers to submit a Senior Officer Core Qualification (SOCQ) Standard—Leading the Intelligence Enterprise (effective October 2010). This SOCQ Standard involves the ability to integrate resources, information, interests, and activities effectively in support of the IC's mission and to lead and leverage cross-organizational collaborative networks to achieve significant mission results. Inherent to this standard is a deep understanding of the intelligence enterprise (or other comparable interagency or multi-organizational environment) and a shared commitment to the IC's core values. There are three competencies that need to be addressed on one page each: 1. Collaboration and Integration; 2. Enterprise Focus; and 3. Values-Centered Leadership.

The **Federal Housing Finance Agency** asks candidates to include a summary, not more than two pages, of experience as it relates to the knowledge, skills, and abilities listed in the announcement. This summary may include professional and volunteer experience, education, training, and awards.

Job announcements from the **Securities and Exchange Commission** request Senior Officer Candidates to submit a resume that integrates the specific knowledge, skills, and abilities, as well as competencies from a set of self-assessment questions, into the resume. The resume may be written similar to the five-page resume-based application for SES. KSAs may include Building Coalitions/Communications; Management Experience; Leading Change/Achieving Results; and questions specific to the position and the agency.

In 2012, the **Department of Defense** will request DoD-specific competencies to be addressed by SES applicants (during a phased approach) demonstrating that they possess the background, ability, and skill to lead across organizational and functional boundaries focusing on the three unique DoD competencies: 1. Enterprise Perspective; 2. Joint Perspective; and 3. National Security.

ECQ: Leading Change
Iraq Nation Building Through Improved Contracting

"When deployed to Iraq, as the Director for Contracting-Forces, subordinate to Joint Contracting Command-Iraq/Afghanistan, I provided overarching leadership for contracting support for 140,000 troops and 12 Regional Contracting Centers, stationed in Iraq and Afghanistan, and executive oversight for more than 5,000 contracts worth $550M, for work including construction, vehicle maintenance, intelligence gathering, media services, and water bottling. Shortly after my arrival, the leader of Multi-National Forces Iraq challenged my organization to take on a more strategic focus; specifically to focus on his strategic objective of improving the Iraqi economy. I accepted the challenge of meeting this objective, but my organization was not immediately ready. My 12 regional centers, while operating well, were largely operating independently of each other, without any integrated focus or standardized procedures—capabilities critical to successful strategic operations. My vision was to create an organization capable of taking on and achieving strategic Theater objectives, while still supporting tactical operations. To realize this vision, I faced numerous obstacles to affect major organizational changes, in an environment of perverse violence and extreme fluidity. The challenges included making changes to operational focus, creating capacity in the organization to take on increased work, developing common processes, and introducing infrastructure changes across the enterprise.

Read the one-page CCAR version of this Leading Change ECQ on page 85.

Chapter Four

Getting Ready to Write

Getting started with a writing project is often the toughest part.

The first step in drafting your SES application is to develop a list of your most significant accomplishments. We call this your "Top Ten List of Accomplishments." Many of our clients and class participants have difficulty developing a solid list of achievements to demonstrate their leadership capabilities. Your goal in this step is to cultivate a variety of examples that highlights the breadth and the depth of your leadership skills and proves that you meet the ECQ leadership competencies.

Assignment: Your Top Ten List of Accomplishments

Brainstorm a list of your significant accomplishments (in a word processing file if possible). For each accomplishment, write a short paragraph to describe it. Do not worry about format at this stage; you are simply trying to generate ideas. In the next part of this book, you will develop your best examples into essays using the CCAR model, which is the OPM-recommended method for writing the ECQs. Aim to have at least 10 solid examples, though it can be helpful to generate as many ideas as possible.

Make sure to list specific projects and programs. You can also include longer-term initiatives or responsibilities. Examples from nonprofit or volunteer activities are acceptable, but they must be leadership examples, such as sitting on a Board of Directors for a large association.

Concentrate on the most recent 10 years. If you have a powerful and relevant example of leadership at the executive level prior to 10 years ago, you may use it as one of your examples, but be aware that the QRB is looking for the most recent examples of leadership to ensure, in part, that the candidate is aware of current events and changes in legislation and policies.

Try to include measurable results for each accomplishment. To get inspired, see the list of sample executive-worthy accomplishements on the next page (in no particular order).

Sample Top Ten List of Accomplishments

To begin developing your Top Ten Accomplishments List, make a list of major, notable accomplishments with far-reaching organizational influence. Use the Leadership Journey chart in Chapter 2 to integrate language into the stories and to learn to write to the specific competencies for each grade level on the journey.

Begin adding challenges, context, actions, and results to your list. Below is an example of an executive level accomplishment using the Challenge, Context, Action, Result model:

#1: Supported the development and implementation of more than 10 disaster bills since 2004. (SES, Leading Organizations)

Challenge: Facing a natural disaster, I had to work quickly to identify funding, and streamline the process of working with numerous individuals and organizations, pulling together a coordinated relief effort.

Context: As the Director of Operations, I focused the development of 30 programs in response to urgent natural disasters around the country. One of the biggest events I responded to was the 2005 Florida hurricane season. The hurricane season displaced 500,000 people over a period of three months.

Action: I coordinated immediate funding to support short-term housing and security programs in Florida. Following the hurricanes, I worked closely with Florida's Deputy Governor to determine the amount and types of federal funds that were available to the state. By working with state auditors and in-house accountants, I developed innovative methods to provide assistance within a very short time frame. For example, I developed two brand new programs that provided early access to funding that was already earmarked for Florida in 2005. The programs allowed state and local officials to immediately meet the needs of their residents.

Result: The new programs I developed in Florida were used as a model for subsequent programs. Since 2004, I coordinated more than $40 billion in total assistance.

Below are nine more accomplishments. They are not yet set up in the CCAR format, but you may be able to identify the CCAR elements. Notice how the examples correspond to the different levels on the Leadership Journey chart.

#2: Established a unit within a newly organized Department of Energy Office. (GS-12/13, Project Management) The Department of Energy, Office of Foreign Investment, conducted a review of foreign investment delivery. Their review discovered some significant gaps in service and resulted in the establishment of the Office of Director of Foreign Investment at the Department of Energy. I was asked by management to set up the policy analysis branch of this new office. I undertook this project and completed all tasks within four months. I developed a timeline of events to ensure that our unit was up and running. It was important to stay on schedule because our unit was required to contribute to a major annual review of foreign projects, which would take place only five months later. I organized the structure of the office, identified roles and responsibilities for individuals deployed to the office, built a strong team of diverse project management specialists coming from various other units, and identified a contractor for a database to support the new office. I participated in the hiring of five full-time employees, as well as soliciting bids and hiring a technology contractor. I received approval from my manager for all project requests.

RESULT: I successfully started the policy analysis unit of the Office of Foreign Investment within the required timeframe. I also coordinated our unit's contribution to the annual review. Since the unit was created, we have received three group commendations from the Director of Foreign Investment.

#3: Led the "Requirements Documentation Team" of a significant A-76 study. (GS-14/15, Managing People & Programs) Analyzing and solving both organizational and operational problems is a major part of my work. Recent consolidation efforts at USAID have presented IT leaders with a number of organizational and operational challenges. USAID has numerous departments and offices around the world; many have their own separate congressional appropriation and often operate with their own separate IT infrastructures and operations. A recent Department of State mandate to consolidate the help desk, e-mail, network infrastructure, and other elements, presented an especially challenging task. I served in a leadership role on several of the committees and workgroups engaged in this activity; most notably two very senior committees, the Administrative Restructuring Advisory Committee (ARAC) and the IT infrastructure working group. These committees were charged with the challenging task of planning and implementing an extensive consolidation, in a very complex and distributed environment, with a very short time frame. Due to my expertise in IT and my ongoing role on the restructuring committee, I was selected to lead the Requirements Documentation Team. I selected and recruited representatives from across the agency to support this effort. We created online groups to coordinate documentation efforts. I held twice weekly meetings and managed to assemble the documents within six months.

RESULT: The A-76 effort was completed and the documentation process was a critical component of the process. I was recognized for my efforts, receiving a special award from the Director.

#4: Answering the President's Management Agenda – E-Gov for the Department. (GS-9/11, Managing Projects & People) I built an electronic management system that met the elements of the President's Management Agenda for E-Gov. This electronic documents system or "e-DOC" was used by the Department as proof that the Department of Justice was "getting to green" on their Office of Management and Budget (OMB) report card for cabinet level agencies. I created the system by expanding a documents system that I was using internally within my office. Initially, I asked my supervisor if the system might work for other offices, and suggested that we initiate a "pilot" test run in another part of the department. After that was successful, I worked with the IT department to implement the system. I submitted a request to obtain funding for one IT employee to work on the project half-time for five months. Adoption rates have been great.

RESULT: Three departments in my organization are now using this new system, and other departments are considering adopting this system. Many employees praised the system in a recent survey.

#5: Served as a member of the Hispanic Executives in Health and Science (HEES) association. (GS-13, Managing Projects) As HEES Secretary, I developed and wrote the charter and created the brief that was delivered to the National Institutes of Health (NIH) Executive Diversity Council (EDC). The EDC commended the goals the charter outlined and the support it pledged to the EDC activities. I introduced online communication tools that allowed Hispanic employees of NIH to develop networks and keep each other informed. Finally, I personally participated on two EDC working groups that addressed the findings of a Diversity study on mentorship and diversity recruiting.

RESULT: HEES now has 84 members and is an active supporter of the EDC goals.

#6: Independently examined and determined need for coalition on training between Army and the Occupational Safety and Health Administration (OSHA). (GS-14/15, Managing Programs) During my formal detail to the US Army, I independently determined that there was a need for the Department of the Army and the Department of Labor-OSHA to jointly cooperate on training of federal personnel. I took on the initiative to develop, draft, and negotiate the signing of an official Memorandum of Understanding and successfully had the document signed and in effect within six months. I also wrote the statement of work for the contractor assisting in the development of the task, and I oversaw the task and contractor's efforts. I also developed changes to the Army Occupational Safety and Health Administrative Manual.

RESULT: As a result of the Memorandum of Understanding that I developed, tens of thousands of Army employees were trained by OSHA.

#7: Created mentoring program in my department. (GS-13/14, Managing Projects & People) I often lead culturally diverse teams, and I am known for building solid, cohesive teams. While I was serving in Japan, my staff consisted of soldiers, Department of the Army civilians, and Japanese local nationals. I took advantage of our location and initiated team building activities during which the Japanese employees of the section were able to introduce us to cultural and historical sites of their country. We shared Japanese traditions, such as the Cherry Blossom Picnic, and introduced the Japanese to American events such as Thanksgiving Dinner. In my current position, my team is recognized as a close, highly effective team lauded for excelling at an array of diverse assignments. I facilitated this positive environment by creating a mentoring program to support younger employees. The program required that each new employee was assigned to a senior member of the staff, who then acted as a Big Brother or Big Sister. I also made time to rotate new employees around the office for two weeks before beginning their full-time assignments. To support knowledge management, I oversaw the creation of an intranet network for my office, as well as a listserv for mentors and mentees.

RESULT: My office has one of the best retention rates in the department.

#8: Led major rulemaking and changing of policies for hazardous waste and emergency response. (SES, Leading Organizations) I planned, prepared and wrote a formal rulemaking on the Department's tasking under Section 1051 of the National Security Authorizations Act including the Advanced Notice of Proposed Rulemaking, the Proposed Rulemaking and the Final rule. I served as principal point of contact and coordinated activities with the White House representative, Congressional representatives and their staff who authored this section of the appropriations bill/law and with the Office of Management and Budget (OMB). I also managed $5.6 million annually to address hazardous waste and emergency response. Over three years, I managed one of the major support contractors and their expenditures in the support of the overall project.

RESULT: The changes to major rulemaking presented a challenge because changes had not been made in 14 years. The negotiations I facilitated were tense, but were ultimately passed by Congress and supported by OMB.

#9: Served as technical expert to facilitate critical communications needs in support of Operation Liberty. (GS-14/15, Managing Programs) I served as deputy chief of the National Intelligence Agency's International Relations division, the office that serves as focal point for all Department of Defense and other federal agencies seeking to obtain secure interoperability of telecommunications and information systems with allies and coalition partners. The terrorist attacks of 9/11 resulted in an increased requirement for secure interoperability with numerous, and non-traditional, coalition partners. My support greatly shortened the time required for providing necessary support to ensure the United States was able to work with its partners and allow for consultation and coordination in near real time.

RESULT: Commended by the field representatives supporting the combatant commanders; I was also awarded the Team Leadership Award, one of only a few in the entire Agency to receive this award.

#10: Created metrics system for accountability and submitted documentation to defend budget requests. (GS-12/13, Managing Projects) I led my office's budget requests from the Office of Management and Budget (OMB), from 2007 to the present. My office operates with an annual budget of $26 million. In order to better measure our results, I initiated a project and developed an internal metrics system. Each lawyer working in my office now calculates the exact number of hours or minutes they spend on each case, which is very unusual for federally employed lawyers. These figures measure our accountability and play a major role in my annual request for funds.

RESULT: Although some staff in the office were reluctant to try the new metrics program, they quickly realized that it benefited them by drawing attention to their accomplishments. Our funding has remained stable since 2007, and using my system, we were able to show senior management in 2009 that the office could not afford cutbacks and still meet our goals.

Exercise: Mapping Accomplishments to the ECQs

After you have developed your Top Ten List of Accomplishments, it is time to begin to match your accomplishments to the ECQs. Below is an exercise to show you how this matching process works.

For each accomplishment below, please select an ECQ that is best demonstrated by that accomplishment. There may be more than one ECQ that fits for each accomplishment, as will likely be the case when you begin to match your ECQs. A suggested answer key is included below.

A. **Leading Change:** Innovation, creativity, vision, strategic thinking

B. **Leading People:** Conflict management, developing others, leveraging diversity

C. **Results Driven:** Accountability, customer service, problem solving, technical credibility

D. **Business Acumen:** Financial management, human capital management, technology management

E. **Building Coalitions:** Partnering, political savvy, influencing, negotiating

Sample Top Ten List of Accomplishments

1. Supported the development and implementation of more than 10 disaster bills since 1998. _____
2. Established a unit within a newly organized Department of Energy Office. _____
3. Led the "Requirements Documentation Team" of a significant A-76 study. _____
4. Answering the President's Management Agenda—built an E-gov for the Department. _____
5. Served as Vice President of the Hispanic Executives in Health and Science (HEES) Association. _____
6. Independently examined and determined need for coalition on training between Army and the Occupational Safety and Health Administration (OSHA). _____
7. In Japan, created "Big Brother/Big Sister" mentoring program in my department among Japanese local nationals, American soldiers, and civilian staff. _____
8. Led major rulemaking and changing of policies for hazardous waste and emergency response. _____
9. Served as technical expert to facilitate critical communications needs in support of Operation Liberty. _____
10. Created metrics system for accountability and submitted documentation to defend $26M budget requests from OMB. _____

Answer Key (Other answers may be possible)
1=A 2=C 3=E 4=D 5=B 6=E 7=B 8=A 9=B 10=D

Mapping Your Accomplishments to the ECQs

On the next two pages, you will practice mapping each of your top accomplishments to one of the five ECQs. Begin by creating a short outline of your top ten accomplishments in the space below. On the next page, fill in the numbers corresponding to the accomplishments that best demonstrate each of the five ECQs.

Some accomplishment examples can be matched to more than one ECQ. This flexibility will help you in your matching. However, if you do not have the right mix of accomplishments to cover the five ECQs, you can revise your accomplishment list to provide better examples for the required competencies.

Note: Your Top Ten List of Accomplishments does NOT have to be in order of importance.

My Top Ten List of Accomplishments Outline

1. _____

2. _____

3. _____

4. _____

5. _____

6. _____

7. _____

8. _____

9. _____

10. _____

If you do not have the right mix of accomplishments to cover the five ECQs, you can revise your accomplishment list to provide better examples for the required competencies.

Top Ten Accomplishments Map

In each circle, write a number from your Top Ten Accomplishments outline. Use the keyword list to decide where each accomplishment fits best.

ECQ 1: Leading Change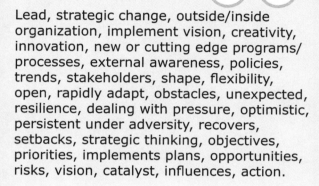

Lead, strategic change, outside/inside organization, implement vision, creativity, innovation, new or cutting edge programs/processes, external awareness, policies, trends, stakeholders, shape, flexibility, open, rapidly adapt, obstacles, unexpected, resilience, dealing with pressure, optimistic, persistent under adversity, recovers, setbacks, strategic thinking, objectives, priorities, implements plans, opportunities, risks, vision, catalyst, influences, action.

ECQ 2: Leading People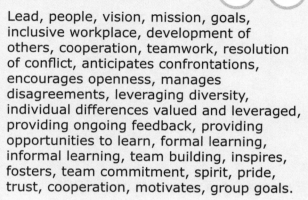

Lead, people, vision, mission, goals, inclusive workplace, development of others, cooperation, teamwork, resolution of conflict, anticipates confrontations, encourages openness, manages disagreements, leveraging diversity, individual differences valued and leveraged, providing ongoing feedback, providing opportunities to learn, formal learning, informal learning, team building, inspires, fosters, team commitment, spirit, pride, trust, cooperation, motivates, group goals.

ECQ 3: Results Driven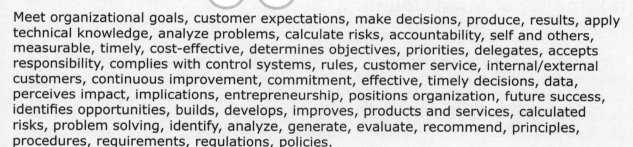

Meet organizational goals, customer expectations, make decisions, produce, results, apply technical knowledge, analyze problems, calculate risks, accountability, self and others, measurable, timely, cost-effective, determines objectives, priorities, delegates, accepts responsibility, complies with control systems, rules, customer service, internal/external customers, continuous improvement, commitment, effective, timely decisions, data, perceives impact, implications, entrepreneurship, positions organization, future success, identifies opportunities, builds, develops, improves, products and services, calculated risks, problem solving, identify, analyze, generate, evaluate, recommend, principles, procedures, requirements, regulations, policies.

ECQ 4: Business Acumen

Manage human capital, financial and information resources, understand financial processes, prepares, justifies, administers program budget, oversees procurement, contracting, achieve desired results, monitors expenditures, cost-benefit, sets priorities, builds, manages workforce, organizational goals, budget, staffing needs, recruit, select, appraise, reward, takes action, addresses performance problems, manages, multi-sector workforce, variety, up-to-date on technology, effective use of technology, ensures access to, security of technology.

ECQ 5: Building Coalitions

Build coalitions, internal, Joint, interagency, other federal agencies, state government, local government, nonprofit, private sector, mult-national, foreign governments, international organizations, achieve common goals, partnering, develops, networks, alliances, collaborates across boundaries, build strategic relationships, political savvy, identifies internal/external politics, perceives organizational/political reality, influence, negotiate, persuade, build consensus, give and take, cooperation, obtain information, accomplish goals.

Excerpt from a successful ECQ

ECQ: Building Coalitions
International Audit Coalition

"I led two multi-location overseas audits, while reviewing the Department of Army's checks and balances intended to detect, deter, and prevent fraud, waste, and abuse in contracting operations outside the USA. To lead this audit, I had to coordinate and develop relationships with Senior Leadership officials from 12 different DoD and Department of Army organizations worldwide. This audit was conducted in Africa and the other team was in Bahrain. All 12 DoD and Army disbursing and contracting Command Activities concurred with the 19 audit recommendations and took immediate action to improve the operations. All six Flag Officers recommended to the Auditor General of the Army the establishment of an audit office in Italy to provide audit coverage for the entire Europe, Africa, and Asia regions. Led completion of the audit in 150 days, 49% less time than normal."

Read the one-page CCAR version of this Building Coalitions ECQ on page 99.

Chapter Five

The Traditional SES Application

In this chapter, we will discuss the specifics of writing each of the components of the traditional SES application:

- Executive Core Qualifications (ECQs)
- Technical Qualifications (TQs)
- Executive federal resume
- Executive cover letter

The bulk of the discussion covers the ECQs, because they are the longest portion of the application, the most difficult to write, and unique to SES.

Step-by-Step Process of Building an ECQ Narrative

Step 1: Use the template, as described and demonstrated in the next several pages.

Step 2: Review the key criteria for the CCAR model.

Step 3: Review the ECQ definition and the leadership competencies for each ECQ.

Step 4: Review your Top Ten List of Accomplishments Map to ensure each example is correctly matched to the ECQ keywords and competencies.

Step 5: Start writing!

Executive Core Qualifications (ECQs)

The most challenging part of the SES application is developing and writing the ECQs. They are narrative statements, written in the first person, that include clear examples demonstrating the competencies and characteristics needed to build executive leadership in a federal corporate culture that drives for results, serves customers, and builds successful teams and coalitions within and outside the organization.

Possession of the Executive Core Qualifications is required for entry to the Senior Executive Service. The ECQs also guide the development of those already in Senior Executive Service positions.

As part of their succession planning, some agencies are also beginning to look for the leadership skills required for executives earlier in the selection process, including using the ECQs in the selection of GS-14 and GS-15 level positions. This is particularly true of selection for agency SES Candidate Development Programs.

Executive qualifications are the primary selection criteria for the SES. While technical job-specific qualifications are important, the essence of the SES is the ability to lead, as articulated in the leadership skills that make up the Executive Core Qualifications. OPM's policy is that ECQs should constitute at least 50%, and preferably more, of the weight when selecting for the SES.

The current ECQs are Leading Change; Leading People; Results Driven; Business Acumen; and Building Coalitions. These ECQs represent a shift from passive management to active leadership. The emphasis today is on innovation, vision, and programmatic shifts that result in organizational change and performance, rather than on managing a process.

ECQ 1–Leading Change

Definition: The ability to develop and implement an organizational vision which integrates key national and program goals, priorities, values, and other factors. Inherent to it is the ability to balance change and continuity—to continually strive to improve customer service and program performance within the basic government framework, to create a work environment that encourages creative thinking, and to maintain focus, intensity, and persistence, even under adversity.

Leadership Competencies

Creativity and Innovation: Develops new insights into situations; questions conventional approaches; encourages new ideas and innovations; designs and implements new or cutting-edge programs/processes.

External Awareness: Understands and keeps up-to-date on local, national, and international policies and trends that affect the organization and shape stakeholders' views; is aware of the organization's impact on the external environment.

Flexibility: Is open to change and new information; rapidly adapts to new information, changing conditions, or unexpected obstacles.

Resilience: Deals effectively with pressure; remains optimistic and persistent, even under adversity. Recovers quickly from setbacks.

Strategic Thinking: Formulates objectives and priorities, and implements plans consistent with long-term interests of the organization in a global environment. Capitalizes on opportunities; manages risks.

Vision: Takes a long-term view and builds a shared vision with others; acts as a catalyst for organizational change. Influences others to translate vision into action.

Writer's Insight

In reviewing the competencies for Leading Change, the definitions clearly reveal that this ECQ is about successfully leading organizational change—it should not be narrow in scope, and it truly needs to focus on "leading change," as opposed to "creating results."

For example, Service Motivation (or customer service) indicates a significant paradigm change for some agencies. Applicants should develop an example in which they have led or significantly contributed to a change in the organization resulting in improved customer service.

Additionally, it is important to tie ECQ responses to current government initiatives. You can easily tie strategic thinking and vision to changing an organization's approach to internal and external customers; this would be considered an example that demonstrates executive level experience. Then, you can tie it to continual learning, since you have learned much about change, and about ways and means to effect change to improve customer service.

CCAR Template

Challenge: What was the organizational change you were trying to lead or direct? What challenges did you overcome?

Context: What were the issues surrounding the change—what barriers were in place to prevent successful change? Who, what, why, when, and where?

Action: What steps did you take personally to lead or effect the change?

Result: What measurable results were achieved? How did you measure them, and how were they recognized? What was the bottom-line change to organizational performance internally and across boundaries?

Example of ECQ Template

Challenge: Changes in management, lack of program commitment, lack of communication, reduced resources, and conflicting priorities.

Context: Within Department of Commerce, program management of energy program had been matrixed with other programs; organization not focused on meeting requirements, old IG findings not taken care of, and lack of program management and direction causing problems with public and other federal agencies.

Action: Developed plan of action and work team to identify issues, prioritize program development and remediation, and develop metrics to measure results.

Result: Program turnaround and improvement, adding value to Department of Commerce and improving public relationships.

KEYWORDS

lead
strategic change
outside/inside organization
implement vision
creativity
innovation
new or cutting edge programs/processes
external awareness
policies
trends
stakeholders
shape
flexibility
open
rapidly adapt
obstacles
unexpected
resilience
dealing with pressure
optimistic
persistent under adversity
recovers
setbacks
strategic thinking
objectives
priorities
implements plans
opportunities
risks
vision
catalyst

ECQ 2–Leading People

Definition: The ability to design and implement strategies that maximize employee potential and foster high ethical standards in meeting the organization's vision, mission, and goals.

Leadership Competencies

Conflict Management: Encourages creative tension and differences of opinions. Anticipates and takes steps to prevent counter-productive confrontations. Manages and resolves conflicts and disagreements in a constructive manner.

Leveraging Diversity: Fosters an inclusive workplace where diversity and individual differences are valued and leveraged to achieve the vision and mission of the organization.

Developing Others: Develops the ability of others to perform and contribute to the organization by providing ongoing feedback and by providing opportunities to learn through formal and informal methods.

Team Building: Inspires and fosters team commitment, spirit, pride, and trust. Facilitates cooperation and motivates team members to accomplish group goals.

Writer's Insight

When developing a response to Leading People, take a moment to reflect on the Leading People competencies.

As you read the leadership competencies, note that each of the leadership competencies highlights the personal actions taken by the applicant—not the actions taken by staff, or through others. The ECQs should focus on your personal contributions that demonstrate how you lead people.

- In leading people, have you coached or mentored?
- What success have you had in the placement and retention of diverse applicants?
- How have you successfully managed conflict in your organization, and what was the organizational effect?

CCAR Template

Challenge: What was the challenge of leading people in this accomplishment/project? What issues did you overcome? Describe the conflict.

Context: Describe your organization and the diversity of your staff.

Action: What actions did you take to lead people through the challenges and to achieve positive change or reach results? Or, HOW did you lead people in this project?

Result: Describe your leadership skills and the results to the larger organization that were achieved by rallying people to follow your vision and meet organizational milestones.

Example of ECQ Template

Challenge: Newly appointed manager of organization with significant issues regarding performance and direction.

Context: Within the Department of Commerce, a decision had been made to "right size" the organization. I came into the position just after actions were completed, and I was faced with meeting organizational goals and objectives with a demoralized workforce.

Action: Met with employees, enhanced listening, did not over-commit to resolve problems, discussed need to move past organizational issues and improve customer service.

Result: Met 100% of organizational goals and, according to an internal survey, increased work satisfaction for nearly three-quarters of the staff.

KEYWORDS

lead
people
vision
mission
goals
inclusive work place
development of others
cooperation
teamwork
resolution of conflict
anticipates confrontations
encourages openness
manages disagreements
leveraging diversity
individual differences valued and leveraged
providing ongoing feedback
providing opportunities to learn
formal learning
informal learning
teambuilding
inspires
fosters
team commitment
spirit
pride
trust
cooperation
motivates
group goals

ECQ 3–Results Driven

Definition: The ability to make timely and effective decisions and produce results through strategic planning and the implementation and evaluation of programs and policies. This core qualification stresses accountability and continuous improvement.

Leadership Competencies

Accountability: Holds self and others accountable for measurable high-quality, timely, and cost-effective results. Determines objectives, sets priorities, and delegates work. Accepts responsibility for mistakes. Complies with established control systems and rules.

Customer Service: Anticipates and meets the needs of both internal and external customers. Delivers high-quality products and services; is committed to continuous improvement.

Decisiveness: Makes well-informed, effective, and timely decisions, even when data are limited or solutions produce unpleasant consequences; perceives the impact and implications of decisions.

Entrepreneurship: Positions the organization for future success by identifying new opportunities; builds the organization by developing or improving products or services. Takes calculated risks to accomplish organizational objectives.

Problem Solving: Identifies and analyzes problems; weighs relevance and accuracy of information; generates and evaluates alternative solutions; makes recommendations.

Technical Credibility: Understands and appropriately applies principles, procedures, requirements, regulations, and policies related to specialized expertise.

Writer's Insight

In responding to Results Driven, describe a management or leadership situation demonstrating personal accountability and commitment to achieving far-reaching results.

In reviewing your work or volunteer experience, select an example where you were challenged to improve customer service, explaining how you used your problem-solving abilities to develop a solution and the decisions you made throughout the process (including those that were unpopular).

Address your technical credibility by demonstrating your ability to achieve results in a large organization or corporation by guiding programs and transformations through administrative and other processes, which may often represent significant challenges in achieving results.

CCAR Template

Challenge: What challenges did you face? What was the condition of the environment that needed changing? What did you identify as needing improvements or overhaul?

Context: Describe the dates, job title, and company name or project—the who, what, where, why, and when of the situation.

Action: What steps did you take personally to achieve results? Use "I" with Actions. Who did you collaborate with?

Result: What measurable results were achieved—how did you measure them, and how were they recognized? Give metrics if possible.

Example of ECQ Template

Challenge: Serious issue in Real Estate Division regarding use and application of professional design services used by the Department of Commerce.

Context: Use of architectural/engineering firms causing problems in costs, use of resources and ability to manage construction, not using advanced building technologies.

Action: Took steps to educate senior management on need for practice changes, benchmarked, and developed action plan to incorporate changes into new building approval process.

Result: Program turnaround and improvement, adding value to Department of Commerce, and improved results, saving the Department millions of dollars.

KEYWORDS

meet organizational goals
customer expectations
make decisions
produce
results
apply technical knowledge
analyze problems
calculate risks
accountability
self and others
measurable
timely
cost-effective
determines objectives
priorities
delegates
accepts responsibility
complies with control systems
customer service
internal/external customers
continuous improvement
commitment
effective
identify | analyze
generate | evaluate
recommend
principles | procedures
requirements | regulations
timely decisions
data | rules
perceives impact
implications
entrepreneurship
positions organization
future success
identifies opportunities
builds | develops
improves
products and services
calculated risks
problem solving

ECQ 4–Business Acumen

Definition: The ability to acquire and administer human, financial, material, and information resources in a manner that instills public trust and accomplishes the organization's mission, and the ability to use new technology to enhance decision-making.

Leadership Competencies

Financial Management: Understands the organization's financial processes. Prepares, justifies, and administers the program budget. Oversees procurement and contracting to achieve desired results. Monitors expenditures and uses cost-benefit thinking to set priorities.

Human Capital Management: Builds and manages the workforce based on organizational goals, budget considerations, and staffing needs. Ensures that employees are appropriately recruited, selected, appraised, and rewarded; takes action to address performance problems. Manages a multi-sector workforce and a variety of work situations.

Technology Management: Keeps up-to-date on technological developments. Makes effective use of technology to achieve results. Ensures access to and security of technology systems.

Writer's Insight

Business Acumen is typically one of the most difficult ECQs to write. The ECQ is very broad, and asks for examples across all aspects of business focusing on Financial Management, Human Capital Management, and Technology. The best way to approach this ECQ may be to identify two or three shorter examples.

Focus on examples describing a management or leadership situation where you demonstrated leadership in at least two of the three required leadership competencies.

For example, you may have provided leadership and direction in the automation of an agency level process or procedure.

You may have managed large scale budgets, in which you were responsible for successful formulation and execution, but you have had to defend requested increases or develop a plan of action when funding levels were not approved.

You may have participated in the development or assessment of human resources tools, such as a new performance evaluation system or other HR tools.

CCAR Template

Challenge: What was the challenge of this business, information technology, or human capital situation, problem, or need? What challenge did you face for the operations or administration of a major program?

Context: Describe the situational background and provide an introductory or overview statement of your ability to manage funds and staffing needs, and to integrate technology into the workplace to create organizational efficiencies.

Action: What steps did you take personally to manage this IT, finance, or human resources challenge, project, or change?

Result: Describe the organizational impact. If the example focuses on finances, then describe in quantifiable results the changes you delivered in terms of saving dollars or restructuring budgets; if the example focuses on human capital/staff, then describe what system you designed to create a strong workforce; and if the example focuses on technology integration, then describe the results of streamlined operations due to the introduction of automation.

Example of ECQ Template

Challenge: Organization required leadership in use of information technology and disposal of 1,000 buildings.

Context: Organization lacked plan of action to effect change in these areas.

Action: Worked with technical staff and senior management to obtain support for changes, and obtained additional funding and resources required to make changes.

Result: Improved use of agency resources and programs, including streamlining operations and gaining efficiencies based on use of automation.

KEYWORDS

human capital
financial
information resources
understand financial processes
prepares
justifies
administers program budget
oversees procurement
contracting
achieve desired results
monitors expenditures
cost-benefit
sets priorities
builds
manages workforce
organizational goals
budget
staffing needs
recruit
select
appraise
reward
takes action
addresses performance problems
manages
multi-sector workforce
variety
up-to-date on technology
effective use of technology
ensures access to
security of technology
social media
e-gov

ECQ 5–Building Coalitions

Definition: The ability to build coalitions internally and with other federal agencies, state and local governments, nonprofit and private sector organizations, foreign governments, or international organizations to achieve common goals.

Leadership Competencies

Partnering: Develops networks and builds alliances; collaborates across boundaries to build strategic relationships and achieve common goals.

Political Savvy: Identifies the internal and external politics that impact the work of the organization. Perceives organizational and political reality and acts accordingly.

Influencing/Negotiating: Persuades others; builds consensus through give and take; gains cooperation from others to obtain information and accomplish goals.

Writer's Insight

The key to this ECQ is the effective development of partnerships and management of key negotiations in support of agency goals and objectives.

OPM is looking for experience in developing and maintaining effective cross-agency, inter-governmental, multi-national, and industry (contractors and academia) relationships to form coalitions and partners that facilitate the greater efficiency, effectiveness, or customer service of the government and to form joint capabilities and information sharing across the globe.

Aim for examples of building coalitions that have stood the test of time. Examples like facilitating or planning an event are usually the least successful.

- Have you built an inter-agency organization?
- Did you cross over agency lines, or reach out to private industry, in order to accomplish a goal or mission?
- How have you improved your organization's performance by working with others?
- Did you lead a group that successfully passed a bill, or have you worked closely with Congress?

CCAR Template

Challenge: What was the challenge of a Building Coalitions situation? Bringing people together often creates divergent viewpoints. What areas needed to be negotiated?

Context: Describe the members (senior leaders by title or organization), the agencies or entities (government agencies, industry, foreign national organizations) of the coalition, and your role within the coalition (leader, member, and contributor). Describe the purpose or need for the coalition. Describe the location (USA, other country, other military service, etc.), and the significance of that.

Action: What actions did you take to build the coalition? Describe your ability to negotiate, influence, or persuade.

Result: What was the result or outcome of the coalition's efforts? Was there a continuing coalition? Describe improved relationships and collaboration.

Example of ECQ Template

Challenge: Limited local infrastructure, no local trust of government or large business institutions, no effective banking system, and obstructionist elements of Iraqi society.

Context: Initiated improvements in the economic situation in Iraq. The objective was to use our contracts to offer business opportunities to the local population.

Action: Held an industry day in the international zone. Coordinated with the US and Iraqi security forces to ensure a safe venue. Partnered with installation leadership to increase the size of a small shopping area that already existed on a base. Arranged a cross-functional team (my staff, the Iraqi government, intelligence and operations officers and security personnel) to begin the process of increasing the Iraqi vendor base.

Result: Developed local small businesses, and built "safe haven" economic zones that resulted in a threefold increase, from 25% to 75%, of contract awards to local Iraqi vendors within six months. Met the strategic regional objectives of improving the Iraqi economy, creating jobs for Iraqi men and women, increasing goodwill, and deterring extremism.

KEYWORDS

build coalitions
internal
other federal agencies
state government
local government
nonprofit
private sector
joint
interagency
multinational
foreign governments
international organizations
achieve common goals
partnering
develops
networks
alliances
collaborates across boundaries
build strategic relationships
political savvy
identifies internal/external politics
perceives organizational/political reality
influence
negotiate
persuade
build consensus
give and take
cooperation
obtain information
accomplish goals

Samples of ECQ Essays

The following ECQ essays are from real case files of The Resume Place (names, locations, and dates have been fictionalized to protect client identities). Some examples include the "before" and "after." As an exercise, review and evaluate each example, identify the problems with each, and examine how those problems were resolved in the final document.

The ECQ essays in this book are one page each. In 12-point font with one-inch margins, that equals about 3,200 characters or a bit less than 500 words. By contrast, two-page ECQ essays can be 4,500 to a maximum of 8,000 characters for various federal online application systems (or two pages maximum for hard copy submissions). Applicants should always be mindful of the specific requirements for different agencies or federal application job boards, as responses/ECQ essays can range from 250 characters to 8,000 characters. You should have a variety of story lengths available for specific job announcements and application types. The CCAR element labels (Challenge, Context, etc.) in these examples are for reference only and should not be included in final essays.

Chapter 6 of this book contains shortened versions of these ECQs for use in the five-page resume-based application format, ranging from about 50 words to 150 words (about 300 to 1,000 characters).

Tip: Even if the announcement indicates that an applicant can use up to 8,000 characters, a shorter and more concise essay response, with powerful, clear writing, is often more attractive to the readers/reviewers than a long, jumbled essay.

Leading Change
1. Delta Air Lines Turnaround Story – Before and After
2. Economic Transformation in Iraq – After only

Leading People
3. Employee Buy-In for Performance Improvement – Before and After
4. Low Team Morale – After only

Results Driven
5. Created a New Organizational Strategy for Agency – Before and After
6. Created Profitable Operations – After only

Business Acumen
7. Secured Location for University-Hosted National Center – Before and After
8. NSPS – After only

Building Coalitions
9. Missile Defense Coalitions – Before and After
10. Audit Coalition – After only

Technical Qualification Samples (3)

ECQ #1: Leading Change

Tip: *Leading Change is about the ability to create and manage multi-agency changes and innovation, which meet the goals, priorities, and values of the organization; it also involves responding to pressure and being flexible under changing conditions. Use a strong opening paragraph that indicates you are in the midst of a big change, without a clear direction for where to go next. Be sure to include "before and after" facts.*

Leading Change ECQ Example 1

Delta Air Lines Turnaround Story (Private Industry to SES)

▶ **Before**

Elected and served as Delta Air Lines' Chief Information Officer and Managing Director Information Technologies in 2005. Led corporate critical division of 1,900 technical professionals organized in two diverse partially owned subsidiaries and an internal department. Working with a mandate to fix past problems with corporate technology, I established and enriched relationships with key users across the company to build plan of action and time frame for the transformation. Results began immediately with significant improvement in the operational efficiency and reliability of the airlines global infrastructure, which provided for greatly improved customer service at airports and reservations offices throughout the world. Additionally, critical applications projects were completed on time and within budget resulting in corporate cost savings and revenue goals being attained. The technology budget was increased during my tenure from $350m to over $550m.

What is wrong with the above essay? Check all that apply

❑ Too short

❑ Does not cover the CCAR format

❑ Misses the Leading Change competency definition

▶ After

(Context & Challenge) As an executive passionately committed to leading change resulting in improved organizational performance, I succeeded in guiding multiple transformational initiatives for Delta Air Lines. As Delta's Chief Information Officer (CIO), I inherited an established division with an operating plan that only covered the next six months of activities. Responsible for Delta's worldwide technology management, I realized that this short-term planning was insufficient for creating value for our stakeholders. My vision was to create a long-term strategy that would stretch the corporate view of the future to a three-year horizon.

(Challenge) Since Delta's planning process was only short term, general in nature, only identified operating expenses and funding for small-scale projects, and capital spending projects were not included and were funded on an "as-needed" basis, I correctly assumed that other operating divisions faced similar challenges. It was evident the company needed to develop a strategic planning process that would address short- and long-term planning, and effectively forecast capital and other expenditures.

(Action) For the IT division, my expectation was simple: create a plan to which people and financial resources could be committed in order to carry out the business objectives of the airline. With 1,900 people in my division and $350M in planned expenditures, I needed to ensure that the IT organization and Delta had engaged in a thoughtful, future-focused process, to ensure that we had identified key strategic and operational objectives, and within that strategy, to ensure effective forecasting and resourcing of projects to enhance our business objectives.

To address this strategic gap, I met one-on-one with my executive peers, which led to a group recommendation to the Chief Executive Officer (CEO) and executive operating council, gaining approval to create the first draft of Delta's strategic operating plan. Technology would be a key driver in the strategy development, based on the potential for efficiencies, the need to deliver on new initiatives to drive revenues, or to achieve cost containment. With approval in place, I wanted to exploit our opportunity for change, and led efforts to the effective design of a strategic planning process. Plan development included the creation and use of a corporate dashboard and metrics. Working with my executive peers, I led the development of and presented the first draft to the operating and executive councils, where we received "hands-down" approval to integrate the strategic planning process as a critical element of the Delta planning regimen.

(Result) I led the development and execution of the first Delta strategic operating plan. Plan development and implementation were integrated into the Delta planning process, providing a consistent process to measure organizational performance and success. The planning process allowed Delta to allocate resources effectively. Initially capital spending dropped by 25%; and use of the strategic planning process allowed Delta to effectively continue to increase its capital spending program, which reached $1.5B.

Leading Change ECQ Example 2

Economic Transformation in Iraq (Military Officer to SES)

▶ After Only

(Context) When deployed to Iraq, as the Director for Contracting-Forces, subordinate to Joint Contracting Command-Iraq/Afghanistan, I provided overarching leadership for contracting support for 140,000 troops and 12 Regional Contracting Centers, stationed in Iraq and Afghanistan, and executive oversight for more than 5,000 contracts worth $550M, for work including construction, vehicle maintenance, intelligence gathering, media services, and water bottling.

(Challenge) Shortly after my arrival, the leader of Multi-National Forces Iraq challenged my organization to take on a more strategic focus; specifically to focus on his strategic objective of improving the Iraqi economy. I accepted the challenge of meeting this objective, but my organization was not immediately ready. My 12 regional centers, while operating well, were largely operating independently of each other, without any integrated focus or standardized procedures—capabilities critical to successful strategic operations. My vision was to create an organization capable of taking on and achieving strategic Theater objectives, while still supporting tactical operations. To realize this vision, I faced numerous obstacles to affect major organizational changes, in an environment of perverse violence and extreme fluidity. The challenges included making changes to operational focus, creating capacity in the organization to take on increased work, developing common processes, and introducing infrastructure changes across the enterprise.

(Action) Time was of the essence; I took decisive action to implement the change. To begin, I challenged my staff to develop an action plan. I then revisited many military combat leaders to explain the changes about to happen. This critical step provided them situational awareness, engendered trust, and obtained their buy-in. I focused the center leaders on the need to standardize processes. I was honest and direct, telling them that the integrity and credibility of deployed procurement operations was on the line; that Congress and the public questioned our ability to make quality business decisions, while still supporting our mission. We agreed to establish a new quality review process to ensure all products met standard. My regional leaders were generally supportive, yet some feared they would not always have capacity to perform tactical AND strategic operations.

(Result) My leadership inspired innovative and creative thinking among my management team. Before introduction of my changes, the organization was not capable of supporting broader strategic initiatives and economic development faltered; after the shift in operations and workloads across the regional centers, we began effectively executing procurement programs to improve/speed the process of economic recovery in Iraq and Afghanistan. Dialogue I engaged in with senior leaders throughout Iraq and Afghanistan, began focusing on both supporting the troops AND strategic economic development. This shift in primary focus completely revamped my organization's role in the region—I began supporting nation building; we addressed NATO issues, grew infrastructure, designated economic safe zones, and built trust amongst the Iraqi business people and public. Overall, I led my organization in delivering a wider range of services, with much broader impact—at the national level, and transformed a tactical operation into a strategic powerhouse.

ECQ #2: Leading People

Tip: Diversity encompasses managing and leading a variety of differences in staff from varying levels of seniority (junior level to senior level/disparate viewpoints/no degree to multiple degrees); a mixture of personnel from various backgrounds and organizations (military, federal, contractors, foreign nationals, expats, industry); age differences (Gen X/Y/Millennials working with Baby Boomers); and varied skill sets (multi-functional teams—from engineers to finance specialists, and skilled/vocational to professionals and credentialed employees) working on the same project. A strong leader of people is capable of motivating teams and managing internal and external stakeholders across industries, disciplines and cultures—in matrix and other organizational structures.

Leading People ECQ Example 1
Employee Buy-In for Performance Improvement (DoD Contractor)

▶ Before

When I began my tenure at DOE in November 2010, the client was extremely dissatisfied with the performance of my predecessor and the existing team. Client satisfaction ratings at that time were 1.0 on a 4.0 scale. Several critical cyber security initiatives were on hold or not bearing fruit for the department, and the CISO and Deputy CISO were not happy with the contractor management. My challenge was to assess the situation, identify the reasons for failure, and quickly implement the necessary changes to get this critical program on track. I spoke with every member of the client and contractor teams in my first two weeks and recognized almost immediately that the majority of the contractor workforce at that time was not aware of the organization big-picture goals and that communication among teams was sorely lacking. Poor communications had created a culture that lacked vision and an understanding of how daily work tied into the client's objectives for the departmental cyber security program.

Lack of sound management discipline and a serious lack of the appropriate cyber security skillets were also the cause of project failure and client dissatisfaction. Upon concluding my initial assessment, I took decisive and immediate action to rectify these deficiencies. Everyone was given an opportunity to perform, and if they were incapable or unwilling to do so, they were moved from the program to other projects. In less than one year, three senior managers and more than ten cyber staff were removed and replaced with high-performing, highly skilled personnel. Within three months of hire, I was recognized by leadership for my efforts at transforming the cyber security team by being promoted from Director of Cyber Security to Associate Vice President with direct reporting responsibility to the Senior VP of Operations, a move that provided me with nearly autonomous control over the cyber contractor program. During these first crucial months, my managers and I were engaged in a complete transformation of our workforce to lead and motivate them to achieve the mission and goals of the Office of the ACIO for Cyber Security by providing staff with opportunities for personal and professional development through the funding and provision of technical and management training and incentives for academic achievements and earning cyber security certifications. We created a culture where employees were valued. This effort to shift the focus to results orientation and build a culture of trust and cooperation among the contractor team produced immediate benefits for our client. Results included:

- Improved communications and reporting, regular meetings among feds and contractors
- Took direct involvement in the management of budgets and resource allocation for all projects
- At the same time providing strategic guidance to the client, I ensured that this strategic vision was communicated to all levels of my staff to include them on the big-picture to motivate them to execute their missions

What is wrong with the above essay? Check all that apply:

❏ Does not meet the definition of Leading People

❏ Bullets and not full paragraphs / narrative writing style

❏ Does not cover leadership

❏ Not in the CCAR format

▶ After

(Challenge & Context) I employ a strategic human resources leadership approach in managing a workforce to achieve maximum growth, productivity, job satisfaction, and a quality work environment, and I inspire people to embrace change. For example, when I began my tenure at DOE, the client was extremely displeased with the performance of my predecessor and the existing team. Client satisfaction ratings were at an all time low (1.0/4.0 scale). Several critical cyber security initiatives were on hold and the Chief Information Security Officer (CISO) and Deputy CISO were dissatisfied with the contractor management. My challenge was to turn around this underperforming organization and put this critical program on track.

My leadership of the contractor change initiative required employee "buy-in" to maximize the potential for successful performance improvement. While I could have simply said, "This is the direction we are going," I wanted this change management process to be different, where staff were inspired by the possibilities offered in the change, recognized the organizational and personal benefits, and were active participants in the process—rather than being "led" through the process. With my innovative leadership, we could engage in a change process where ideas were valued, and staff were motivated to surface their own ideas for change, resulting in a collaborative transformational process that would benefit all staff involved in the change.

(Action) To achieve this goal, I designed a variety of employee engagement forums to share my vision, and led discussions with large and small groups and individuals, seeking ideas for change, commitment and opportunities to promote inclusion and participation. Using this approach, and conducting these forums in a collaborative manner, I was successful in opening communication channels and establishing a continuing dialogue on change management, functional suggestions and opportunities. Within this environment, the staff and I worked together to openly evaluate the "value add" of change suggestions, and determine which ideas were practical and executable. Some of the dialogue was challenging. I applied sensitivity in addressing past performance; however, I was able to manage these conversations effectively, addressing conflict at the earliest stage, without impact to our process. These conversations became a foundational element of our change and contributed significantly to accelerate the change management process, meeting DOE requirements with increasing effectiveness.

(Result) Because of my leadership and willingness to address these issues directly, after several months, attitudes began to change; staff began to work together and challenge one another to excel. This change resulted in timely completion of projects, tripling of customer satisfaction ratings, and recognition of the team's positive attitude by other managers. I wanted to ensure that these changes were effectively recognized, implementing a new focus on award and recognition for teamwork, knowledge sharing, and improved customer service. I highlighted teamwork in meetings and with customers. Overall, my leadership has resulted in improved staff performance, customer service, morale, and long-term retention.

Leading People ECQ Example 2

Low Team Morale (Industry to SES)

▶ After Only

(Context) In my most recent assignment as Executive Vice President of Consumer Goods USA in Long Beach, California, my headquarters' staff was composed of personnel from two US regions, the Headquarters, and members from two countries. This comprised the management team and the mid-level staff. I quickly recognized that the management team handled their direct-reports in a very hierarchical, depreciative manner, manifested in a chasm between the management team decision-makers and the mid-level staff. This resulted in low morale, self-esteem and motivation on the part of the middle management staff, accompanied by a very high level of complaints and personnel turbulence.

(Challenge) I, at the same time, recognized in my mid-level staff much talent and potential. With the amount of work and challenges in the current business across the USA and in five other countries, plus my intent to quickly enter other unexploited markets; combined with a need to support the integration into our business of a newly acquired and refurbished plant, I urgently needed to unlock the potential of my mid-level staff and give them autonomy to perform to their potential. I also needed to impose my will on the current management team, to demonstrate to them the benefits of a more enlightened, inclusive approach to managing their people, yet at the same time not alienate them and thus lose sorely needed momentum in our business operations.

(Action) I accomplished this by officially establishing a "leadership team" composed of the management team and their direct-report mid-level managers. I officially inducted the new members of the leadership team and briefed them on their duties and obligations as leaders in our company. They attended my periodic management team meetings. The new members participated enthusiastically, taking the initiative and offering sound proposals to business issues, volunteering to lead projects and otherwise demonstrating that they were indeed leaders.

(Result) We were now addressing more issues and projects simultaneously than previously. The morale of my new leaders improved noticeably, and this enthusiasm cascaded to the entire organization. My management team welcomed the increased momentum in the organization and increasingly trusted and empowered their staffs. I reinforced my new leaders' role and my trust in them by direct personal contact without having to directly involve their management team supervisors.

To capitalize on my initial success and to fully establish the new leadership team, I scheduled an off-site meeting three months later to inaugurate the upcoming annual and strategic planning process. I directed that the meeting be prepared and conducted by the new leadership team members, who presented the current business status and their proposals to the management team. This extremely successful meeting fully institutionalized the new leadership construct. I smoothly achieved a fundamental and enduring transformation to a leadership culture of inclusion, empowerment, trust and teamwork. The Region showed markedly improved morale and reduced personnel turbulence. We attracted the best candidates as our organization expanded to support our business growth and market expansion.

ECQ #3: Results Driven

Tip: It is easy to use a Project Management slant for Results Driven, which can become a process-oriented story. However, the QRB is looking for a 60,000-foot view of a leader's ability to focus and lead an organization to produce results. Be sure to include plenty of actions and results from the executive level, avoiding a narrower focus; include quantifiable results to system improvements. Use opening and closing paragraphs that highlight why improving results was critical to the organization's mission.

Results Driven ECQ Example 1
Created a New Organizational Structure for Agency (Federal to SES)

▶ Before

Holding various positions within the federal government, I have a proven track record of getting results through people and sound management. For example, in my current piston as the Director of Workforce Planning and Management, Congress directed my Agency in Fiscal Year Conference Reports to "improve the management of FTE's, including forecasting, tracking, and monitoring the agency's FTEs. The committees also stressed disappointment with the agency's management of FTEs and suggested that continued mismanagement with no longer be tolerated. I recommended to the Agency that the FTE management program be transferred from the Budget Office to my office to ensure all inclusive Workforce Planning efforts. I also ensured him that I would fix the FTE management problem and improve our relationship with Congress. My request was granted and I won approval from the Appropriations committee to realign these functions to my office. Once the realignment was completed, I met with staffers from both the House and Senate (weekly) to gain a better understanding of their issues and concerns about our agency.

After analyzing the FTE issue and evaluating the current process, I discovered that the agency was hardly managing FTEs and was using an excel spreadsheet for tracking purposes. The agency was also severally underutilizing our FTES, had prematurely placed the agency on a hiring freeze, and was uncertain about how positions and FTEs were actually recorded. To correct the FTE management problem, I first reviewed the current and historical FTE reports, reviewed the spreadsheet maintained by the Budget Office, and evaluated the 10 appropriations and their associated FTE Caps and utilization. I then reviewed the current methodology for forecasting FTEs and concluded that the methodology was flawed and did not project end-of-year FTE utilization correctly. I immediately developed a new methodology for forecasting and monitoring FTEs.

> **What is wrong with the above essay? Check all that apply:**
>
> ❑ The story lacks results
> ❑ Project management oriented, as opposed to leadership oriented
> ❑ Spelling and grammatical errors

▶ After

(Challenge & Context) As the new Director, Workforce Planning and Management, I learned that employees were complaining that their grade levels were inconsistent across the Agency, leading to numerous Equal Employment Opportunity complaints. As a result, several managers began meeting with me to discuss options for "reorganization" and methods to resolve the perceived problems with the grade levels. In addition, EEO had contacted me to discuss grade disparities across the Agency and asked for my advice on how best to address the "poor perception" and the concerns of employees and managers across the agency. To address these challenges, I initiated an Agency-wide review of the organizational structure. During this review, I requested (and was approved) from the Agency head to put a moratorium on all organizational changes until the study was completed. I approved and recommended disposition for all Agency-wide position actions, organizational actions, and any issues relating to the organizational structure of the Agency.

The study revealed that the Agency did not have a consistent organizational structure, supervisory ratios varied for like functions, grade levels were incorrectly classified, and inappropriate elevated divisions and inappropriate levels of management (the organizational structure) were driving the grade levels for positions (which appeared to be the root problem). I took a global review of how the Agency was structured, grouping organizational entities by work functions and mission. The analysis revealed that the Agency, as a requisite, needed a consistent structure and appropriate functional groupings.

(Action) Working with the Employee and Classification Branch under the Human Resources Division, I held high-level meetings with managers, supervisors, and senior level management to convey and diagram the inconsistencies and inherent problems with the organizational structure, the cause of their growing problems, and gain their buy-in for the newly proposed Agency-wide organizational structure (that would result in consistency across all organizations). This was a politically charged issue across the spectrum of employees; therefore I determined a plan of action to eliminate internal and external (our stakeholders—Congress) problems.

(Result) I designed a politically sensitive strategy and transformed the entire organizational structure resulting in a drastic reduction of EEO complaints (from 11 to one), the elevation of numerous positions to appropriate grade levels, and a future plan for reducing grade levels that were incorrectly classified. My strategy ensured that current employees were not monetarily affected by the decrease in grade levels, supervisory levels were not reduced until attrition occurred, and employees were briefed on the changes and were explained the "benefits" of the new structure (winning support—even if their grade was negatively impacted). I provided focus for a communication plan for stakeholders (Congress) explaining the new changes, remaining sensitive to negative or disparate assumptions. The organizational structure and full strategy that I proposed was approved by the Agency, the Senate and House Appropriations Committees, and the EEO and HR Divisions, and was implemented in FY10.

Results Driven ECQ Example 2

Created Profitable Operations (Industry to SES)

▶ After Only

(Context) As a business leader and military officer, I routinely formulate and manage business and operational plans for the organizations I lead, including staffing plans for hundreds of personnel in many offices and plants across five countries and administration of operational and marketing budgets up to $20 million. I create highly profitable strategic plans for my company.

(Challenge & Context) When appointed General Manager, Consumer Goods USA at the Headquarters in Long Beach, California, I was challenged to turn around a business that had been hemorrhaging cash for the previous two years due to lackluster leadership and no strategic business focus. Despite the company's purchase of two plants with capacity to fulfill more than 20% of market demand, the domestic organization and business had not been properly developed. High-margin premium brands were handled by an exports division, depriving the local market of much-needed profits to fund investments to grow the organization and build the domestic business. In addition to these daunting business challenges, I assessed the plants' staff as lacking motivation, drive, and initiative. I essentially faced a "start-up" situation.

(Action) Within two months, I developed a strategy to address the personnel and business issues I faced. My immediate focus was improving the staff's attitude and professionalism to establish the right corporate culture as the organization expanded to develop the domestic market. In parallel, I aligned the organization behind key business processes focused on the development of the domestic market, which I established as the number one priority for the entire organization. I initiated a hiring and sales training program that produced a trained and ready domestic sales force that went from 10 to 70 employees in only four months. I streamlined and grew the distributor network from one to 10 in a six-month period, ensuring national distribution of our brands. I streamlined the locally produced brand portfolio, discontinuing low-volume brands, thereby achieving manufacturing efficiencies and focusing sales and marketing activities behind strategic priority mid-price brands.

(Result) These actions demonstrated to corporate leadership that I had set the conditions for a robust domestic sales and distribution organization. I easily achieved transfer to my control of the high-margin premium brands that were managed by the export division. I instituted sales and marketing programs to fully align and motivate the staff, the sales force, and the trade behind the newfound total brand portfolio concept. Within six months, the company doubled its sales volume with domestic sales. This achievement resulted in record-high sales volume. Just as important, the company showed a profit for the first time in three years. Additionally, I implemented other cost saving measures that brought an immediate savings of $5 million to the company; overall I created a very successful consumer goods market in the USA.

ECQ #4: Business Acumen

Tip: Use one or two stories that cover all three of the competencies for Business Acumen (Financial Management, Human Capital Management, and Technology Management). Your example should integrate all the aspects of business management. Recruitment is also important; OPM looks for creative management. For example, using detail assignments for temporary employees, or acting under tight deadlines.

Business Acumen ECQ Example 1

Secured Location for University-Hosted National Center for Forensic Science (Federal to SES)

▶ **Before**

I am a seasoned senior manager, with an established record of success in leveraging utilizing resources effectively. Resource management is critical to the success of any organization; creative resource management can make or break an organization in today's cost-conscious, streamlined environment. My success in managing resources was demonstrated when I led the planning required to secure a location for the University- hosted National Center for Forensic Science.

The University of Central Florida had been newly designated as host of the National Center for Forensic Science. Funding was available for the Center's computer forensics mission set, but not for separate and distinct office space or a facility. The University, in its proposal to host the Center, had noted anticipated synergistic benefits of co-locating this Center alongside other federal, state university, and private sector entities with expertise in simulation, modeling, and training that could be applied to computer forensics.

As a strong leader, I believed I coud obtain a state-funded facility on federal land in exchange for office space for federal employees. I supervised a team to brainstorm ideas and determine if, and how a joint-use facility could be constructed on located property. I built consensus and develop a proposal, which I presented to obtain the necessary approvals. My presentations to all stakeholders focused on the untapped opportunities to create synergy among public and private partners to position the state to be increasingly competitive in attracting federal funding. Under my leadership, the necessary approvals were approved. I also coordinated with appropriate staff and elected officials to obtain approval for state appropriations to cover construction costs.

My leadership resulted in the construction of a joint-use public-private facility dedicated to simulation and training, public safety, and forensic science.

What is wrong with the above essay? Check all that apply:

❏ This essay is short

❏ It does not address the full CCAR format

❏ It includes a "belief"

▶ After

(Introduction & Context) My success in leveraging and utilizing resources effectively was demonstrated when I spearheaded a challenge to lead the planning required to secure a location for the University-hosted National Center for Forensic Science; the University of Central Florida had been newly designated as host. Funding was available for the Center's computer forensics mission set, but not for separate and distinct office space or a facility. The University, in its proposal to host the Center, had noted anticipated synergistic benefits of co-locating this Center alongside other federal, state university, and private sector entities with expertise in simulation, modeling, and training that could be applied to computer forensics.

(Challenge) Finding a positive solution for the facility, including facility funding for a consolidated center of excellence, would be a challenge. Military partners noted constraints of no available office space and a 10-year horizon for new military construction (MILCON). University officials could not identify vacant property or office space. Private sector partners were not able to develop solutions acceptable to legal review.

(Action) To address this challenge, I envisioned a state-funded facility on federal land (no-cost lease) in exchange for office space for federal employees. I led a team to brainstorm ideas, work through barriers, and find solutions. To energize the team around a potential solution, I had identified 12 acres of vacant federal land nearby. I guided the team to determine if, and how, a joint-use facility could be constructed on this property. I led all efforts to develop a proposal to obtain the necessary approvals. My presentations to all stakeholders focused on untapped opportunities to create synergy among public and private partners to position the state to be increasingly competitive in attracting federal funding. Under my leadership, the necessary approvals from Congress, State of Florida, University, DoD, DOJ, Navy Facilities and Engineering Command, Research Park authorities, local regulatory bodies, and others were approved. Simultaneously, I coordinated with appropriate staff and elected officials to obtain approval for state appropriations to cover construction costs. Unanimous approvals were granted, principals signed binding agreements, and planning for the facility began.

(Result) My leadership, creativity, and tenacity resulted in the construction of a joint-use public-private facility dedicated to simulation and training, public safety, and forensic science. Tenants included the National Center for Forensic Science, Naval Air Warfare Center Training Systems Division offices, university research laboratories, offices, and training rooms available to local public safety professionals. I had the foresight to obtain advance authority to facilitate streamlined lease amendments for any future facilities construction. My collaborative efforts to champion teams to bring innovative concepts and ideas to reality has led to continuous partnering and growth among public and private partners with simulation and modeling expertise. Today, three Partnership Buildings populate the once vacant site.

Business Acumen ECQ Example 2

NSPS (Federal to SES)

▶ After Only

(Context) In a response to a directive to convert General Schedule to the new National Security Personnel System (NSPS) for the Army Audit Service, (Action) I designed and implemented human capital strategies to meet organizational mission and goals. I led and focused a five-person Process Action Team (PAT) established to develop performance and developmental expectations, policy, and procedures to fully implement the National Security Personnel System (NSPS) for the Army Audit Service. (Action) Through my leadership on the Process Action Team, I guided my team in full development of the framework of human capital strategies to ensure Army Audit Service achieved these NSPS goals. For example, my vision included the creation of standardized performance plans for all three pay band levels, for each career field, for 1,200+ auditors and support personnel, aligned with the Army Audit Service mission and strategic goals. Army Audit Service Senior Leadership approved the use of the performance plans and Task Assignment Agreement forms to fully implement NSPS at Army Audit Service. My Process Action Team developed this automated system designed as a program management tool.

(Challenge) Our organization was part of the first wave to transition from the GS to the NSPS performance-based system in the Department of the Army, so leading this effort was unique and challenging. Since this type of work had never been done in our organization, I led with a flexible attitude to meet our hard deadline and to have all the performance plans and tools in place to implement the NSPS performance-based system. My team met with other Federal Audit agencies that had performance-based rating systems to obtain ideas and lessons learned to provide guidance in developing these new tools, business rules, and policies to implement NSPS.

(Result) I successfully guided my team in meeting the due date, and management approved the performance plans, procedures, business rules, and tools. I achieved our Strategic Objective of implementing an effective and efficient NSPS performance-based plan. All 1,200 auditors attended all NSPS training, and 100 percent of supervisors performed and documented required employee feedback sessions. In addition, I was able to terminate seven poor performers, through use of this new tool, obtaining full endorsement from the Human Resources Officer and the assigned attorney.

In my NSPS performance rating, which received the highest rating of "5," my supervisor wrote, "Because of his exceptional leadership skills in developing solutions to respond to new issues, he was handpicked to lead the Army Audit Service process action team that developed the performance plans and tools to successfully implement NSPS."

ECQ #5: Building Coalitions

Tip: Building Coalitions reaches far beyond coordinating events and delivering speeches. Rather, it is about the need to create strong, focused coalitions with internal and external entities to promote the sharing of information and creation of harmony across boundaries. Make certain that the reader understands that you are working out program issues at senior levels in the organization. Also, demonstrate your ability to nurture lasting, long-term relationships.

Building Coalitions ECQ Example 1
Missile Defense Coalitions (Military to SES)

▶ **Before**

I believe this is my strongest area. It is most definitely the area I enjoy most, provided leading and working with people is integral. Team building, partnering and communications, both verbal and written, are extremely important to effective organizations. I have spent over 30 years in the military working in and improving on all these very skills. I have extensive experience leading and developing working relationships within organizations on up to interagency levels. I have worked with Congress and on Congressional actions, building personal political savvy that takes years to develop. I also have vast experience nurturing relationships, developing and enhancing alliances and engineering coalitions across a wide range of interests and cross-functional activities that includes extensive international work with our friends, allies and business partners.

During my time on the USEUCOM staff, I not only honed my U.S. political savvy during this period, I grew experience in international political savvy as well. Much of the experience I have related above and the evaluation quotes previously provided directly attribute to my coalition building and effective communication skills. However, to add some more specifics I will provide more evaluation comments:

"Difficult period in a difficult command dispersed over three geographic areas yet still able to coalesce his team to provide ever increasing support at all levels, including NATO and Joint Service Commands, significantly improving support and quality of life for all."

"My Number One of 44 Officers of all designators including two more senior."

"The finest Naval Officer it has been my pleasure to command. The Number

One officer of 45 assigned, including four more senior. Recognized bedrock of the community. Equally adept at handling the concerns of Flag Officers and E-1's alike."

"Keynote speaker… Commencement speaker… Community spokesman…

Always out front at every community event. Superb written and oral communicator."

"Highly lauded team builder who inspires cooperation. Promoted a positive working climate within a diverse group of people across all directorates in his host command. Built a superb team of missile defense experts who will represent warfighter interests for years to come. Recognized throughout USSTRATCOM as the MDA expert. His efforts as the single point of contact at the MDA representing USSTRATCOM and the entire mission area of Global Ballistic Missile Defense (GBMD) has been near heroic. He has developed dozens of personal and hundreds of professional relationships through innovative methods that have notably enhanced unit cohesion and directly improved command climate between two very large organizations. His ad hoc team leadership and sheer breadth of situational awareness regarding missile defense actions means his expertise and honest broker opinion is sought after by all. His unprecedented personal initiative, combined with his mature seasoned Pentagon and political savvy, have been critical toward accomplishing the President of the United States National Security Directive to accelerate and "operationalize" GBMD."

"A gifted leader...superb handling of Joint Staff and Congressional staffs...outstanding reputation throughout EUCOM, Theater Component Commands, NATO/SHAPE staffs, Joint Chiefs/OSD Staff Officers and Congressional Staff Members." "A charismatic leader... superb leadership of his 50-member Congressional Issues Team through the fast-reaction, high pressure testimony cycle...outstanding leadership with CINC/DCINC/Component Commander/ NATO and U.S. staffs during more than 90 CODEL visits comprising 354 Members of Congress [during a one-year period]...Community Leader and Core Values Ambassador." "Key community leader. Elected as the J-5 Directorate CMEO [Command Equal Opportunity Officer]. Absolute role model of fairness and respect. Recognized pro-active community EO leader."

What is wrong with the above essay? Check all that apply:

❑ The original essay is jumbled with quotes from performance evaluations

❑ Filled with acronyms

❑ Unfocused

❑ Not in the CCAR format

❑ Too long

▶ After

(Context and Challenge) I was working at the Missile Defense Agency (MDA) as the sole military representative for US Strategic Command when the President issued a National Security Presidential Directive ordering the DoD to take all measures necessary to field an initial Missile Defense capability within two years.

(Action) US Strategic Command (USSTRATCOM) served as the military advocate for DoD. Using transformational policy that I helped to write, USSTRATCOM was given the mission of "Global" [strategic directly linked to theater] Missile Defense and authority as the primary military interlocutor to the MDA. I guided the design, building, and implementation of a coalition between USSTRATCOM, the Pentagon staff (including the Military Services) and the regional Combatant Commands; establishing formal policy, processes, and procedures for conducting military Missile Defense operations. I also built a lasting coalition for continued research, development, and acquisition for Warfighter Involvement Process.

(Result) Prior to the deadline, under Presidential authority, the Secretary of Defense declared Initial Defensive Operations for the Ballistic Missile Defense System (BMDS). I was awarded a Joint Service Achievement Medal for my actions leading to this declaration and a Defense Meritorious Service Medal for my achievements while serving as the USSTRATCOM Representative to the MDA.

(Sub-story) I also built a solid coalition between the National Reconnaissance Office (NRO) and the MDA, which is expanding to other Intelligence Community (IC) organizations. For more than five years, there has been a direct relationship between the MDA and the NRO; however, no documents codifying this relationship existed when I began working at the NRO. I drafted and staffed an overarching Memorandum of Agreement (MOA), which was ultimately signed by the Director NRO and Director MDA. That MOA serves as the keystone document for myriad engagements and formal [funded] projects between these two organizations. Subsequently I authored, at the NRO's request, the MDA Engagement Plan. These engagement plans act as the NRO's primary strategic communication outlining and directing activities between major coalition partners. I briefed my MDA Engagement Plan to an approving board, which was accepted with minor changes. My plan was ultimately approved and placed into final staffing process for NRO Director signature in January 2011.

Building Coalitions ECQ Example 2

Audit Coalition (Federal to SES)

▶ **After Only**

(Context) As the Audit Director, I led an audit to coordinate and develop relationships with Senior Leadership officials from 12 different Department of Defense (DoD) and Department of Army Commands and Activities worldwide. This audit was conducted in Djibouti, Africa (acquisition audit) and the other team was in Bahrain (disbursing audit). This was particularly difficult, as we were only allotted 150 days to complete the audit work on-site, 49 percent less time than is standard to complete this type of audit.

(Challenge) No operating agreement existed between the Command and Activities, which created a "turf battle" over who had ultimate accountability and responsibility for the key contracting and disbursing functional areas. This created confusion amongst the Commands in terms of who would perform the corrective actions relating to audit findings and recommendations. As such, I remained sensitive to the political landscape in leading this multi-location audit.

(Action) I initiated communication with senior military (Joint) managers for each of the key functional areas to address roles and responsibilities to eliminate confusion and duplication of services. I networked with colleagues from their parent Commands to identify solutions and gather information on "best practices" for managing similar joint operations with multiple commands and activities. I shared this information with the senior military managers and recommended the establishment of a working group to clarify roles and responsibilities; to determine the best contracting and disbursing organizational structure to support their strategic mission; and to respond to our recommendations. There were serious conflicts among the groups as to what the report should address and the direction of recommendations. As the overseer, I often mediated the disputes. I briefed six Flag Officers from the major commands to gain their support, and obtained their full endorsement before the report was issued.

(Action) The working group/coalition was established with the 12 DoD command and activities, and from this working group's recommendations, the Department of Defense established my organization as the Executive Agent for providing contracting and disbursing support to the sites. This eliminated the confusion as to who should respond to the audit findings and recommendations, and the "turf battles" between the commands. Due to my leadership, 19 recommendations were presented to the consortium that included: change business practices and processes and reduce disbursing and contracting operation risks; improve the efficiency and effectiveness of disbursing and contracting operations; and strengthen the integrity and adequacy of these checks and balances to prevent fraud, waste, and abuse.

(Result) All 12 DoD disbursing and contracting Command Activities concurred with the recommendations and took immediate action to improve the operations. All six Flag Officers fully endorsed the audit, praised the report results, and recommended to the Auditor General of the Army the establishment of an audit office in Naples, Italy to provide audit coverage for the entire Europe, Africa, and Asia region.

Technical Qualifications

Technical Qualifications (TQs) are executive level "knowledge, skills, and abilities" (KSAs) required by agencies and identified on job announcements. They may also be called the Mandatory Technical Qualifications (MTQs), Mandatory Technical Competencies (MTCs), or Professional Technical Qualifications (PTQs). TQs are specific to the position and agency, and may be written as separate one-page essays addressing each TQ for a traditional executive federal resume and ECQ application package, or integrated into a five-page resume-based application (per the job announcement). Candidates will be required to demonstrate experience and skills sufficient to successfully perform the duties and responsibilities of a particular executive level position by describing superior technical qualifications and technical knowledge.

Many executive positions have specific subject-matter knowledge and skill/competency requirements that candidates must meet. The TQs are competencies that agencies may identify specific to the position being filled. Well-written TQs indicate a required level of proficiency in a functional area. The examples/accomplishments/stories used for TQs need to express executive level proficiency.

The TQs are drafted in the CCAR format, like ECQs, for the traditional essay package; they can be reframed and used as short summary paragraphs, integrated into the five-page resume-based application. TQs describe functional areas of expertise, and can be used as screen-out factors for HR specialists and hiring managers. Hiring managers are seeking highly qualified candidates who have current knowledge of a specific subject matter. So use recent stories (within the past 10 years), describe expertise directly related to the TQs, and use the language/keywords from the TQs and the duty description section of the job announcement within the TQ narratives.

Avoid using laundry lists. Some candidates believe that the TQs are less important and they spend less time developing the TQ responses; however, the hiring agency is very interested in a candidate's TQs to help score knowledge, skills, and abilities. TQs can be similar stories to ECQs, if a TQ is the same or has nearly the same requirements as an ECQ. For example, if a TQ reads: "Describe any experience you have supervising and/or managing personnel in the accomplishment of major projects, please include the nature and scope of the work supervised," you may be able to draw from a story you developed for Leading People and rewrite the story with a different point of view—focusing on the agency's needs and other specific requirements gleaned from the vacancy announcement.

TQs may need to be rewritten for varied job announcements, as the qualifications may not be the same for each announcement; whereas ECQs often can remain static, because they are focused on specific leadership competencies. TQ bullets may also need to be replaced on a five-page resume-based application, tailoring the resume to the specific TQs from a different announcement.

Technical Qualification Samples

Example #1:

Describe experience in formulating, developing, implementing, and revising policies, strategies, and processes for national security programs related to natural or other disasters and emergency response.

(Challenge) A post-Katrina evaluation of FEMA's hurricane response caused changes to be made to align all federal agencies to one National Incident Management System (NIMS). The Air Force Incident Management System (AFIMS) was created to mirror NIMS as the AF emergency response structure. I was challenged to align the old response organization, its people, processes, and structure to the new system. This involved reorganizing how medical, safety, law enforcement, fire, caregiver, and command and control responded to emergencies, were allocated and managed, to best target and maximize the response. My vision was to revamp the process and build an organization with a broader focus that could handle multiple emergencies effectively.

(Context) Supporting a large Air Force base (AFB), I led a 1,700-person organization operating the base infrastructure. Additionally, I was the On-Scene Director for the Disaster Control Group, leading responses to real-world and simulated emergencies in a 14-state region.

(Action) I began building relationships beyond the installation to provide broader community support. I visited state Emergency Management Agencies (EMA) meeting with directors and detailing my plans for a collaborative effort. I also visited the local Army National Guard to establish mutual support agreements for transportation, airlift, explosive ordinance and biological/chemical support. I dispatched medical experts to local hospitals to establish emergency support agreements. I revised on-scene command and control. To prepare these mid-level leaders to lead during a wide range of emergencies, and to communicate effectively with the higher-level Emergency Operations Center (EOC), I worked with emergency response stakeholders to create realistic, multi-scenario training simulations. During repeated exercises, first responder leadership and communication skills dramatically improved.

As the EOC Director, I created an installation EOC to provide command and control, funded the construction necessary for the EOC to operate, and directed the renovation of the communication suite to ensure contact with first responders in the field. The EOC managed all aspects of an emergency including first responder oversight; state and local liaison; media inquiries; higher level reporting requirements; and reported directly to senior installation leadership. I also created space within the EOC for state and local agencies to operate.

(Result) I guided the transformation of the organization's emergency response apparatus from a traditional, locally focused, disaster control element, to a nationally oriented emergency management machine, merging Air Force, state and local emergency response agencies into one powerful emergency management operation, capable of managing multiple events, while effectively coordinating response actions, with many internal and external stakeholders. I established an AFIMS-compliant EOC in just eight months, 33% ahead of schedule. My actions elevated the AFB to national level compliance and provided a broader, more effective capability for the Air Force. For actual and follow-on simulated emergency situations, I reduced the response time needed to establish multi-event command and control by approximately 15-30 minutes—a significant improvement in this critical, life-and-death, time-sensitive environment.

Example #2:

Experience in developing and implementing organization-wide operations and processes for deployment, security, and oversight of large scale technology services, and leading broad cultural change in information technology management roles.

(Challenge) I faced the challenge of persuading numerous Agency law enforcement components to support the Law Enforcement Information Sharing Program by publishing shareable law enforcement information that could be accessed by other federal, state, local, and tribal law enforcement agencies via databases.

(Context) As Deputy Director for e-Gov and Information Sharing in the Office of the Chief Information Officer, I was hired to execute the program. The Law Enforcement Information Sharing Program (LEISP) is the Agency's program to share law enforcement information routinely across jurisdictional boundaries to prevent terrorism, and to systematically improve the investigation and prosecution of criminal activity. The LEISP is a program focused on changing the culture of law enforcement information sharing from "need to know" to "need to share."

(Action) I began by working with colleagues and contractors to focus the reallocation of resources so a data distribution facility could be designed, developed, and deployed within existing budget thresholds. The LEISP data distribution facility was designed to support the publishing and distribution of more than 100 million records. Once built, the facility allowed the Department's law enforcement components to publish shareable law enforcement information to be shared with one or more technology-based information sharing systems.

Second, my senior colleagues and I established a governance framework to monitor the execution of the Law Enforcement Information Sharing Program strategy and compliance with policies promulgated by the Deputy Attorney General. I co-led the LEISP Coordinating Committee (LCC) with the Deputy Attorney General, and provided oversight of the large law enforcement information effort. During meetings, I briefed the LCC metrics on the law enforcement components compliance, describing law enforcement information to be shared in the system.

Third, I guided development of a process to engage state and local law enforcement agencies to create law enforcement information sharing partnerships, including getting local US Attorney and Agency law enforcement field office support. The process I designed also included steps to ensure state and local law enforcement agencies could adhere to prescribed security guidelines and requirements for vetting users who would view the Agency's law enforcement information.

(Result) My work to execute LEISP led directly to a dramatic expansion of shareable law enforcement data from 22 million records to more than 60 million records, and an increase in state and local partnerships from six to more than 32. My leadership of this process enabled well over 2,900 federal, state, local, and tribal law enforcement agencies to enter into productive nationwide information sharing partnerships across the broader federal law enforcement and intelligence community.

Example #3:

Experience in developing and implementing organization-wide operations and processes for advanced engineering and manufacturing operations and addressing specific needs or challenges.

(Context) As Corporate Vice President of Engineering, I led an Enterprise Resource Planning (ERP) upgrade to meet Sarbanes-Oxley compliance for the corporation (with 27 plants across the nation, and plants in Mexico and Japan), with annual revenue more than $1.2 billion. I was recruited to assume the additional responsibility to bring three separate operational structures into one, joining the corporation under one Product Engineering (R&D) Division.

(Challenge) When I joined, the corporation had not met or passed Sarbanes-Oxley compliance in two years, it did not have any policies in place for guidance within the ERP system, and many different functional areas were overlapping into other functional areas of responsibility. The lack of procedural guidance caused great confusion; manufacturing had control of costing and labor routings and standards; purchasing was able to change suppliers without following Engineering Procedures for approval; any staff had access to engineering Bill of Materials and could change parts, routings, and material requirements at will; and purchasing had capability to change raw material or component cost without approval or costing by accounting.

(Action) I formed a senior working group including the Director of Information Systems, Director of Accounting, Director of Manufacturing, and Director of Customer Service to develop and write policies to ensure compliance with Sarbanes-Oxley and create an entire "chain of command" and flow chart to ensure departments managed their own assigned functional responsibilities. The newly documented policies and procedures prevented duplication and lost items, and ensured streamlined processes and a standardized process for each department across the corporation, plus it eliminated any functional area or person to have access that would create a conflict of interest. I focused the working group's writing of the new policies, which I presented before the Executive Management Council and Board of Directors for unanimous approval. I then introduced my vision and strategy for rollout of the new policies.

(Challenge & Action) Overseeing this transformation was a challenge. I encountered strong resistance in some functional areas, and I worked with senior managers to solve pushbacks and defuse animosities. Due to the reestablishment of authority levels, all departments corporate-wide were involved in the changes to ensure compliance with Sarbanes-Oxley. Under my direction, the leadership staff developed and implemented a comprehensive training program for corporate-wide implementation including webinars and presentations/awareness meetings to smooth emotions and gain consensuses across the corporation, at all levels, and within all the functional departments. I personally traveled to all sites to meet with leadership.

(Result) Guiding a team of senior managers at all sites, all departments adopted and implemented the new processes. During an inspection, only three months after implementation, the entire company met inspection requirements—the first time ever that the corporation met and exceeded the Sarbanes-Oxley requirements. The transformation was so successful, my program was requested as a model process for other interested corporations, and I was the invited guest speaker at the Association of Executive Manufacturers.

The Executive Federal Resume

The executive federal resume is used for applying to GS-15 and SES announcements and is prepared in the federal resume format. It may be submitted via a formatted (hard copy) document or an online resume builder; we suggest that you have both versions ready and then follow the instructions on the announcement. This resume is on average three to five pages and must include relevant Work Experience (from the last 10 years), Education, Certifications, Awards, Relevant Training, and accomplishments that demonstrate your leadership skills.

The ECQs and TQs do not need to be covered in the traditional format executive federal resume. However, the short accomplishments identified in the executive federal resume should be stories used in the ECQ essays. The HR professionals will verify and cross-reference that the stories you use in your ECQ essays are identified on your resume.

Executive federal resumes include more detailed descriptions of work experience, focusing on the most recent 10 years and summarizing positions held prior to 10 years ago. This resume usually includes a short executive profile highlighting your most notable career achievements including the largest number of personnel you supervised, the largest budget you managed, your interactions with very senior level people, your overall ability to influence positive organizational performance on a far-reaching scale, and perhaps the addition of a notable award or very important career achievement.

The resume should be drafted in reverse chronological order. It may include a brief description of each organization's operational scope (the size of the organization and its mission), combined with a short description of your leadership (duties), and a short list of bulleted accomplishments (key leadership initiatives) with results for each position. Accomplishments demonstrate your past performance and your knowledge, skills, and abilities needed for the position. When the organization's mission is noted, it is easier for you to describe within the context of your accomplishments how you led programs to meet the organizational mission and goals.

A careful analysis of an announcement and the major duties will reveal key words and competencies that the HR professionals are seeking to qualify a candidate for a position. As you review an announcement, highlight keywords and themes within the position description and TQs, and integrate those words and themes into the achievements listed on your resume.

For example, if a duty description from a vacancy announcement is focused on leading a large staff and managing large budgets, then your resume will need to reflect your ability to lead large staffs and focus on fiscal management. If the announcement is focused on interacting with Congress and other senior level stakeholders in government and developing policy, then you will want to include examples that demonstrate your work with Congress and the development of policy for your organization, company, or agency. Use the major duties and TQs from a job announcement as a guide for developing the content of your resume.

Here is an example of identifying keywords and skills from an announcement for a Financial Services Director:

The incumbent exercises **executive leadership** in the following areas: **Principal advisor** who provides **authoritative advice** to the Director for **Fiscal Operations** and **Policy** and other officials, with policy and **operational advice** and **counsel** dealing with **financial, strategic initiatives and operations issues** affecting **Domestic Finance** and other Departmental **policy offices**.

Relationship Management. Provides direction and **guidance** to **financial agents** to **deliver identified services** and quickly **respond to changing circumstances**.

Provides **Management oversight** for the **financial agents** designated to provide services for programs throughout the Departmental Offices.

Directs a subordinate staff in **managing relationships** with financial agents on a daily basis, serving as a **central point of contact** for both the financial agents and the agency program offices that rely on the financial agents' services. The incumbent also **manages staff effectively** to enhance each individual's **professional development**.

Develops and issues policies to financial agents to **execute and support large, complex financial transactions**.

Provides **advice** on the broad **range of Federal fiscal operational** and policy issues.

Provides **advice and guidance** to **improve use of automation**.

The keywords and skills that are required and sometimes repeated in this announcement are bolded above. These are the words a candidate who is applying for this position would use to integrate into the resume.

Here is an example of how the keywords and skills may be integrated into content for a resume focused on the applicant's specific leadership scope:

As the Deputy, **Financial Operations**, I lead a **subordinate staff of six direct-report supervisors managing relationships** for a multi-functional team of 28 including **financial agents**, analysts, and administrative staff supporting 2,000 customers in 10 different offices spread across the nation.

Policy advisor to senior leadership for **fiscal operations** and **policy** development, responsible for presenting to the Agency Head and Congressional Budget Office a $4B adjustment to agency expenses in FY12.

The executive federal resume is one part of the entire SES/ECQ/TQ application package. It is part of how you present yourself to the hiring staff. You will want the entire application to be the best quality by presenting your qualifications well. Write with the audience in mind (the HR professional, hiring manager, ERB, and QRB) using clear, concise, active, and executive language.

Checklist of do's and don'ts to prepare a highly competitive executive federal resume:

Do:

- Use 12-point font and one-inch margins
- Include the announcement number on the resume
- Use recent, notable achievements, and quantify and qualify results
- List recent education, advanced training, or new credentials to enhance your qualifications
- Spell out acronyms in the first instance
- Use a combination of short paragraphs and bullets
- Ensure the resume expresses overall executive leadership experience
- Use a strong writing style that emphasizes leadership competencies, technical qualifications, and major accomplishments with results
- Carefully analyze the announcements for major duties, keywords, TQs, and competencies required for the position
- Tailor each resume submission to meet the needs of the new vacancy announcement

Don't:

- Use too many bullets
- Use the big block style of writing (large blocks of text without breaks or bullets)
- Mix fonts or use fonts that are too small to read
- Describe personal beliefs or philosophies

See executive federal resume samples in the case studies in *Chapter 9 Sample SES Applications*.

See the rest of Judy Johnson's case study, including the background, before resume, USAJOBS resume, and cover letter in Chapter 9 starting on page 148. Judy's five-page SES federal executive resume can be found in Chapter 6 starting on page 116.

JUDY JOHNSON

Permanent:	Judy@gmail.com
5420 Constantine Avenue, Washington, DC 92865	Cell: 555.202.4986

Citizenship: US	Social Security Number: xxx-xx-5555

Announcement Number: SES-2011, Executive Director, Mobilization & Training, Dept. of Navy

EXECUTIVE PROFILE
• • •

Senior executive with full oversight direction for strategic planning and business leadership for large, geographically separated organizations, hundreds of employees and multi-million dollar operating budgets, while holding dual careers with multi-national, fast-moving consumer goods corporations, and in leading US Army organizations. Develop policy and regulatory compliance. Culturally acclimatized, politically correct, and diplomatic; excellent political-military skills. Structure joint operations.

• • •

EXECUTIVE INDUSTRY EXPERIENCE
Consumer Goods USA, 20-YEAR CAREER

Executive Vice President	**10/2009 - Present**
Long Beach, CA	**Salary: $150K per year**
Supervisor: Mr. Tom Hansen; 555.349.2940; Contact: Yes	**Hours per week: 60**

* Consumer Goods USA is an international consumer goods business with 25,000 employees in 20 countries.

Implemented a strategic vision for business operations and development in the USA region of this international company with offices in 20 countries. Indirectly supervise an office staff of 65 and sales force of 80, with dotted-line supervision to 175 plant workers, and independent distributors across five countries. I manage cross-cultural issues, enforce EEO regulations, and create programs to heighten morale and foster diversity. Manage an operational budget worth $7.9M. Empowered and coached staff with low morale, gained trust, and energized a very talented management team and their direct reports to exceed their potential.

Major Accomplishments:

- Integrated the brands, employees, distributors and business operations of a major company acquisition in 2009.
- Achieved annual and strategic plan (3-year planning horizon) volume and profit targets.
- Ensured full integration of new plant in Long Beach. Melded marketing and sales organization from east coast for office support (Finance, IT, Logistics, Legal & HR) and ensured cooperation between HQ marketing and sales departments, HQ R&D and Global Supply Chain.

Vice President, Corporate Marketing Initiatives   06/2005 - 10/2009
Cincinnati, Ohio   Salary: $140K per year
Supervisor: Mr. Donald Anderson: 495.874.9230; Contact: Yes   Hours per week: 40

Corporate-wide single point of contact for regulatory compliance and initiatives. Developed and implemented Direct Marketing vision, strategies, programs and budgets. Supervised 100+ staff and administered $47M marketing budget. Articulated regulatory market instructions for Annual & Strategic Plan HQ instructions. Introduced technology and led large-scale projects.

Major Accomplishments:
- Built coalition and actively managed the Regulatory Compliance Working Group in creating strategic and contingency plans for corporate response to regulatory trends.
- Guided development of and achieved the on-time, on-budget implementation of a corporate-wide consumer products directive, which saved the company $45 million over five years.
- Led implementation of corporate-wide Internet-based direct marketing pilot program.

Vice President, Imports   12/2003 - 06/2005
Long Beach, CA   Salary: $105K per year
Supervisor: Mr. James Smith; 555.349.7811; Contact: Yes   Hours per week: 40

Oversight supervision for senior staff of 28. Directed multi-functional team of operations in five countries. Managed all aspects of importation of $70M sales of high-margin premium and sub-premium brands. Reported to Regional President as member of Regional Executive Committee.

Major Accomplishments:
- Successfully negotiated and managed disengagement from importers, thwarting importer strategy of multi-million dollar cash extraction and disturbance of commercial operations.
- Managed full project management lifecycle of multi-functional operations team of plant R&D, HQ Packaging, and marketing & sales staff to ensure synchronized Product, Packaging, Operations Planning, Marketing and Selling activities.
- Secured return of bank guarantees of $28 million via successful negotiations with customs authorities.
- Successfully redeployed key managers via intensive personal networking, as well as coaching / mentoring and exposure via delegating direct responsibility for projects.

Earlier Position
General Manager, Consumer Goods USA, 1998 - 2003 (Long Beach, CA)
- Complete P&L responsibility for more than $100M in domestic sales, distribution and marketing of products manufactured in two local plants and imported from five countries. Reported to Regional President. Directly supervised 19 director-level staff and office staff of 60 at the HQ office. Oversight direction for 120-strong field sales force and 2,000 plant employees across the USA.

US Army (Active & Reserve Components) Experience, 1985 - Present

Major General, US Army Reserve
Deputy Chief of Staff, Headquarters
Europe
Supervisor: John Jones; 555.398.3800; Contact: Yes

05/2005 - Present
Salary: $25K per year
Hours per week: 30

Principal advisor to Commanding General, US Army Europe on all Reserve Component affairs and activities. Monitor processes for training and readiness of the Reserve Component. Liaison between multiple military components for development of plans, policies and procedures for training support and contingency operations. Oversight leadership for 1,200 Soldiers and civilians and 21 divisions. Organizational representative at meetings, events, and exercises. Unique additional leadership oversight includes:

Major Accomplishments:
- Spearheaded US Army Reserve Schools Initiative in Europe, increasing interoperability by teaching US military doctrine to foreign military partners.
- Appointed Deputy Exercise Director for the next Fiscal Year's major exercise, which entails mentoring an active component Major General (senior officer) and leading the ground force activities of the Joint Exercise Control Group.
- Led two major Army and Air Force exercises. Supervised and guided a multi-service staff team and multiple Army and Marine organizations in planning and execution as part of a US-led Joint Task Force operating in a sovereign host nation.

Major General, US Army Reserve
Deputy Director Planning, Washington, DC
Supervisor: Jerry Winters; 555.497.4488; Contact: Yes

01/2002 - 05/2005
Hours per week: 40

Advised Director, Strategic Plans in support of Chairman, Joint Chiefs of Staff top calendar issues for defense plans and programs. Expert at annual NATO Crisis Management exercise. Represented the Office at international conferences, Joint Staff Talks, and other events.

Major Accomplishments:
- Senior US military representative at US Department of State-led conferences and negotiations. At Proliferation Security Initiative conference, participated in negotiations with foreign contingent to achieve tangible commitments to this critical undertaking.
- Guided diplomatic negotiations gaining respect of allied hosts. Directly contributed to Mexico's decision to begin Joint Staff Talks; led the annual Joint Staff Talks with Chile.
- Developed first-ever Host Team Leader brief delineating Host Team activities that were synchronized with pre-established inspection timelines. This brief was incorporated into Host Team standard procedures.

Brigadier General, US Army Reserve
3rd Army Reserve Command, Germany
Supervisor: Andrew K. Myers; 202.555.2002; Contact: Yes

07/1995 - 01/2002
Hours per week: 40

Led a major subordinate command of United States Army Europe, composed of 34 units and 2,000 Reserve and Active-duty Soldiers, and civilian employees. Administered and executed an operating budget of ~$30M. Supervised 15 direct report subordinate managers. Fully accountable for ensuring subordinate units were manned, trained, and maintained a high rate of readiness for mobilization.

Major Accomplishments:

- Realigned force structure to meet the evolving needs of the total Army. Initiated an annual force structure review process with HQ and its major subordinate commands.
- Instituted a routine mobilization preparedness regimen for all units including enhanced measures in response to 9/11 to ensure personnel and unit mobilization readiness.
- Implemented Equipment Storage Site-Expanded concept, producing a validated 97% equipment serviceability rate from previous 75%, in just one year.
- Outsourced logistics, increasing by 25% the time for units to focus precious training time on their core competency: mission operations.

EDUCATION & US ARMY PROFESSIONAL MILITARY EDUCATION

- **Master of Business Administration**, University of Maryland, 1998
- **Bachelor of Science in International Relations**, University of Virginia, 1987
- **National Security Management Course**, National Defense University, 1998
- **US Army Command and General Staff Officer Course**, 1997

PUBLIC SPEAKING ENGAGEMENTS

- "US Army Europe in Transformation." Delivered speech in German, 2011
- American Chamber of Commerce Serbia, and Serbian and international press. "Update on International Operations and Investments in Serbia," Serbia, 2009
- Press conference, UN Palace of Nations, Geneva, Switzerland, 2008

Conferences / Symposia

- Annual Serbia and Albania Economist Intelligence Unit conferences, 2000 - present
- First Annual Proliferation Security Initiative Conference, Warsaw, Poland, 2009

OTHER

Languages: German 3/3 • French 3/3

Military Awards & Decorations:

- Legion of Merit
- Defense Meritorious Service Medal
- Meritorious Service Medal
- Army Commendation Medal
- Army Achievement Medal

Clearance: TS/SCI

The Executive Cover Letter

A cover letter or letter of interest may accompany a senior executive application package to help a candidate stand out. Make sure to follow carefully the vacancy announcement requirements; some agencies request the inclusion of a cover letter with an SES application package, while other agencies indicate that they will only accept a resume or other specified documents, and will not review any documents beyond those specified.

The purpose of a cover letter is to describe the applicant's interest in the position and to reemphasize qualifications consistent with the vacancy announcement; it should not simply restate the content of the resume. If the letter is written well, the HR staff will glean prominent qualifications from your application that are most critical to the advertised position, and you may build some rapport with the reader. Leverage the cover letter to highlight brief examples of how your experience is a strong fit for the position, and to illuminate convincing leadership qualifications essential to the open position. Structure the cover letter to help you stand out among even the fiercest competition.

The cover letter components may include:

1. **A header** that matches the header of a formatted federal resume. Preparing a standard header that can be used for all of your presentation resumes, cover letters, ECQ essays, and other documents will create a theme and a professional appearance.
2. **Short leadership highlights or bullet points** to affirm information contained within the resume/application. Bullets points break up the page and help the reader's eye to zero in on specific achievements or points of interest.
3. **An explanation of transferable skill sets** if you feel you are only minimally qualified in a leadership or technical competency. For example, if you are experienced in all ECQs and TQs, but lack specific knowledge of an agency-specific regulation, yet you are familiar with an equivalent regulation from your agency or company, then you may use the cover letter to describe the equivalent level of knowledge and how it might translate to the target agency.

It is important to personalize and address each cover letter to the individual listed on the vacancy announcement. Be certain to identify the announcement number, position title, and a list of attachments for each application. Each letter should be concise, targeted to a specific position, energetic, and positive, and it should describe to the reader the executive contributions you can make.

The cover letter can be one to one and a half pages, with one-inch margins and the same font used for the resume (in 11- or 12-point). The cover letter may be uploaded to USAJOBS or Application Manager (as a formatted Word document), as needed, or used as an email attachment or hard copy. For online systems, you will want to convert the cover letter content to a text file and copy and paste it into the appropriate federal builder. Follow the instructions for specific character lengths.

See executive cover letter samples in the case studies in *Chapter 9 Sample SES Applications* on pages 159 and 173.

ECQ: Building Coalition
Missile Defense Coalitions

"I built a solid coalition between the National Reconnaissance Office (NRO) and the Missile Defense Agency, which is expanding to other Intelligence Community (IC) organizations. I drafted and staffed an overarching Memorandum of Agreement [MOA], which was ultimately signed by the Director NRO and Director MDA in 2010. That MOA serves as the keystone document for myriad engagements and formal [funded] projects between these two organizations."

Read the one-page CCAR version of this Building Coalitions ECQ on page 98.

The New Five-Page SES Federal Resume

Creating Your Five-Page SES Federal Resume

Your challenge in writing the five-page resume will be to describe up to 20 years of experience and include evidence of the ECQs in the text of the resume. The final product will be a coherent five-page document that tells a story of senior leadership by covering all 28 leadership competencies, but not actually identifying the ECQ categories. The 2010 Guide to SES Qualifications by OPM states: "Candidates should keep the ECQs in mind as they write their resumes, but it is not necessary or even advisable to annotate the resume with 'Leading Change', 'Leading People', 'Results Driven', 'Business Acumen', or 'Building Coalitions.'" ECQ labels in the SES resume samples in this book are for reference only.

TIP: The evaluators are looking for demonstrated evidence of your ECQs and the leadership competencies woven throughout the entire five pages.

The five-page SES federal resume should be written with one-inch margins and 12-point font. It may need to be copied and pasted into USAJOBS or another federal resume builder, uploaded as a Word document into USASJOBS or Application Manager, or submitted as a Word attachment via e-mail or hard copy package to be mailed. In all cases, it should not exceed the five-page limit.

By now, you should have completed the following:

- Created your top ten list of accomplishments
- Written your accomplishments in the CCAR format
- Written your traditional format federal executive resume, ECQ essays, and cover letter

If you have already completed the above, then creating your five-page resume will be fairly simple. Even if you have not completed those steps, you should be able to create your five-page resume.

Step 1: Create Short Accomplishment Bullets

Edit your ECQ and TQ narratives (or top ten list of accomplishments if you have not yet written your ECQs) into short, five- to eight-line bullets or paragraphs. If you are not able to use the full CCAR format for an example, then focus on the accomplishment and the result. Try to highlight a challenge, a context, and an action in at least one of your examples in order to demonstrate the full range of your leadership strengths.

Step 2: Resume Template

Using the sample five-page resumes from this book as models, create a similar template outline in your word processing program. Prepare the header with your name, address, phone, email, and the announcement number. Set up topical headers throughout the document: Executive Profile, Experience, Education, Training, Awards, Publications, or other specific topics related to your background or the announcement. Alternatively, if you are converting a traditional federal executive resume, save the file with a new name and use the headers and work experience headings.

Step 3: Writing the Work Experience Section

Job Headers: In the Work Experience section, set up the employment blocks in reverse chronological order, starting with your most recent employer and moving back in time. Include the company or agency with city and state, full dates (months and years for start and end dates), hours worked per week, salary, and a supervisor's name and phone number.

Leadership Duties: Include a short overview of your company's mission and scope of services, followed by a brief description of your leadership duties. The leadership duties become the "Context" from the CCAR from your ECQ stories.

Bulleted List of Accomplishments: Following the leadership duties, include a bulleted list of short accomplishment statements from step 1. Your resume should highlight ALL of the ECQs and TQs required on a job announcement. To help make sure that you cover all of the requisite ECQs and TQs, identify each bullet in your draft as an ECQ or TQ (Leading Change, Leading People, Results Driven, Business Acumen, Building Coalitions, and so forth), and remove the identifier when you perform your final edit.

It is not necessary to include multiple accomplishments under each work description. However, you do want to ensure that all the ECQs and TQs are addressed within the most recent 10 years, maximizing the use of a variety of diverse stories. You may need to shorten education, training, awards, and other sections to provide additional space for the ECQ and TQ accomplishment bullets.

How Your Five-Page SES Federal Resume Will Be Scored

The resume-based application process is considered a screening method, to be used in conjunction with a structured interview. The evaluators will review all background materials including the vacancy announcement, position description, leadership and technical qualification competency definitions, and relevant benchmarks. They will review the resume materials, evaluate the resume, and assign a rating. The evaluators will identify the executive leadership experience considering the complexity of the position or situation, scope and breadth of the results or outcomes, and the time horizon (how the result affects future issues or events).

For a candidate to be qualified in the Top Group/Highly Qualified and recommended for an interview, the evaluators must identify full mastery of the ECQs and TQs.

When writing the resume interwoven with ECQs, remember to avoid generalities and use specifics that describe the complexity, scope and breadth, and time horizon of your story:

BEFORE (Does NOT demonstrate full mastery): *Customer-oriented Agency expert for IT responsible for end-user satisfaction at all levels. Report to the Agency Head concerning all issues related to IT and innovation.*

AFTER (Demonstrates full mastery): *Oversight leadership for supporting IT requirements for six operating Divisions supporting 10 major programs in three countries. Direct and focus the priorities of 900 personnel and administer a $150M budget. Introduced strategy and associated management approach to transform the Agency's legacy systems, expanding information sharing 30%.*

The after example provided enough detail to show "evidence" of executive leadership, and it provided a "picture" of the scope of leadership and management responsibility of the candidate.

See the rest of Judy Johnson's case study, including the background, before resume, USAJOBS resume, and cover letter in Chapter 9 starting on page 148. Judy's paper version federal executive resume can be found in Chapter 5 starting on page 107.

JUDY JOHNSON

Permanent:
5420 Constantine Avenue • Washington, DC 92865

Judy@gmail.com
Cell: 555.202.4986

Citizenship: US
Social Security Number: xxx-xx-5555
Announcement Number: SES-2011, Executive Director, Mobilization & Training, Dept. of Navy

EXECUTIVE PROFILE
20-year Corporate Career / Senior Sales & Marketing Executive / Consumer Goods USA
Major General, US Army Reserve (1989 - present)
Multi-lingual: German & French • TS/SCI

• • •

Senior executive with full oversight direction for strategic planning and business leadership for large, geographically separated organizations, while holding dual careers with multi-national, fast-moving consumer goods corporation headquartered in Long Beach, California, and in leading US Army organizations in Europe. Develop policy and regulatory compliance. Culturally acclimatized, politically correct, and diplomatic; excellent political-military skills. Structure joint operations to include deftly leading foreign consequence management operations.

• • •

EXECUTIVE INDUSTRY EXPERIENCE
Consumer Goods USA, 1989 - Present

Executive Vice President
Long Beach, CA
Supervisor: Mr. Tom Hansen; 555.349.2940; Contact: Yes

10/2009 - Present
Salary: $150K per year
Hours per week: 60

Implemented a strategic vision for business operations and development in the USA region of this international company with offices in 20 countries. Indirectly supervise an office staff of 65 and sales force of 80, with dotted-line supervision to 175 plant workers, and independent distributors across five countries. I manage cross-cultural issues, enforce EEO regulations, and create programs to heighten morale and foster diversity. Manage an operational budget worth $7.9M.

Key Leadership Initiatives:

- Integrated the brands, employees, distributors and business operations of a major company acquisition in 2009. *(Business Acumen)*

- Achieved annual and strategic plan (3-year planning horizon) volume and profit targets. *(Results Driven)*

- Empowered and coached a diverse staff with low morale; gained trust and energized a very talented management team and their direct-reports to exceed their potential. Led a headquarters' staff in Long Beach composed of personnel from two US regions, the Headquarters, and members from two countries. This comprised the management team and the mid-level staff. The management team handled their direct-reports in a very hierarchical, depreciative manner, resulting in many complaints and personnel turbulence. To establish the new leadership team, I scheduled an off-site meeting and directed that the meeting be prepared and conducted by the new leadership team, who presented their proposals to management. This successful meeting institutionalized the new leadership construct and I achieved a leadership culture of inclusion, empowerment, and teamwork. The HQ staff showed markedly improved morale and reduced personnel turbulence. *(Leading People)*

- Ensured full integration of new plant in Long Beach. Melded marketing and sales organization from east coast for office support (Finance, IT, Logistics, Legal & HR) and ensured cooperation between HQ marketing and sales departments, HQ R&D and Global Supply Chain. *(Building Coalitions)*

- Developed, agreed upon, and implemented a strategic vision for Consumer Goods USA's business operations across the nation and the plants in 20 other countries to standardize operations reflecting 5- to 10-year assessment of regional trends including Free Trade Agreements; market regulatory trends; trade evolution; and competitive strategies. Incorporated relevant elements into annual and strategic business objectives, plans, programs and budgets, including organizational and business mode shifts. *(Leading Change)*

Vice President, Corporate Marketing Initiatives
Cincinnati, Ohio
Supervisor: Mr. Donald Anderson: 495.874.9230; Contact: Yes

06/2005 - 10/2009
Salary: $140K per year
Hours per week: 40

Corporate-wide single point of contact for corporate marketing and regulatory compliance and initiatives. Developed and implemented Direct Marketing vision, strategies, programs and budgets. Supervised 100+ staff and administered $47M marketing budget. Articulated Regulatory market instructions for Annual & Strategic Plan HQ instructions.

Key Leadership Initiatives:
- Formed and actively managed the Regulatory Compliance Working Group in creating strategic and contingency plans for corporate response to regulatory trends. Ensured that financial and commercial impacts of directives were incorporated into Headquarters and individual market operating and strategic plans. *(Business Acumen)*

- Guided development of and achieved the on-time, on-budget implementation of a corporate-wide consumer products directive, which saved the company $45 million over five years. Compliance with the directive was named a corporate priority for the upcoming three-year period, as the out-year's corporate budget planning was already underway, and thus would have visibility with the Board of Directors. *(Results Driven)*

- Led implementation of corporate-wide Internet-based direct marketing pilot program, which was so successful that it was adopted corporate-wide and expanded to cell phone coverage and social media. *(Business Acumen)*

Vice President, Imports
Long Beach, CA
Supervisor: Mr. James Smith; 555.349.7811; Contact: Yes

12/2003 - 06/2005
Salary: $105K per year
Hours per week: 40

Reported to Regional President as member of Regional Executive Committee. Supervised senior staff of 28. Managed all aspects of importation of $70M sales of high-margin premium and sub-premium brands from five countries.

Key Leadership Initiatives:
- Successfully disengaged from importers, thwarting importer strategy of multi-million dollar

cash extraction and disturbance of commercial operations. *(Business Acumen)*

- Directed multi-functional team of operations in five countries: R&D, HQ packaging, plant, and marketing and sales staff to ensure synchronized product, packaging, operations planning, marketing and selling activities. *(Leading People)*

- Secured return of bank guarantees of $28 million via successful negotiations with foreign customs authorities, as well as rigorous project management of simultaneous product disposal and excise stamp recovery operations in two major cities. *(Business Acumen)*

- Successfully redeployed key managers via intensive personal networking, as well as coaching/ mentoring and exposure via delegating direct responsibility for projects. *(Leading People)*

Earlier Position
General Manager, Consumer Goods USA, 1998 - 2003 (Long Beach, CA)
- Complete P&L responsibility for more than $100M in domestic sales, distribution and marketing of products manufactured in two local plants and imported from five countries. Reported to Regional President. Directly supervised 19 director-level staff and office staff of 60 at the HQ office. Oversight direction for 120-strong field sales force and 2,000 plant employees across the USA.
- *Turned around a business that had been hemorrhaging cash for previous two years.* Rallied organization behind vision statement. Achieved control of imports of high-margin premium brands formerly managed by Export Department. Instituted sales/marketing programs to fully align and motivate staff, sales force and trade behind the newfound Total Brand Portfolio Management. Closed two plants, securing $12M in cost savings. *(Business Acumen)*

US Army (Active & Reserve Components) Experience, 1985 - Present

Major General, US Army Reserve   **05/2005 - Present**
Deputy Chief of Staff, Headquarters   **Salary: $25K per year**
Europe   **Hours per week: 30**
Supervisor: John Jones; 555.398.3800; Contact: Yes

Principal advisor to Commanding General (Director-equivalent), US Army Europe on all Reserve Component affairs, activities, and policy development. Monitor processes for training and readiness of the Reserve Component to meet security and force protection objectives. Liaison between Commanding General, US Army Europe and Chief, Army Reserve and Director, Army National Guard for development of plans, policies, procedures, and guidance for coordination and synchronization of Reserve Component integration into US Army Europe peacetime training support, as well as contingency operations. Represent leadership at exercises, conferences and other activities involving Reserve Component personnel and issues, to include distinguished visitors to the US Army Europe area of responsibility.

Key Leadership Initiatives:
- Oversaw two major Army and Air Force exercises. Led a multi-service staff and multiple Army and Marine organizations in planning and execution as part of a US-led Joint Task Force operating in a sovereign host nation. Guided senior staff in determining the personnel strength required for both combat and post-combat phases; setting the Theater for port, airfield and basing needs; coordinating flow in and staging of forces and materiel; conducting ground combat operations, synchronizing with Air Force, Navy and Special Operations Forces

counterparts; managing immediate post-combat stability and humanitarian relief operations, as well as redeployment of US forces and transition of the land forces mission to the host nation and international organizations. *(Leading People/Results Driven/Business Acumen)*

- As a result of successful performance, appointed Deputy Exercise Director for the next Fiscal Year's major exercise, which entails mentoring an active component Major General (senior level) and leading the ground force activities of the Joint Exercise Control Group. *(Leading People)*

- Deputy Chief of Staff, Operations, US Army Europe for several months. Oversight leadership for 1,200 military personnel and civilians and 21 divisions, supporting war plans, training, exercises and international operations for 70,000 Soldiers in US Army Europe; as well as the deployment and redeployment of US Army Europe units and individuals to Iraq and Afghanistan for Operations Enduring Freedom and Iraqi Freedom. *(Results Driven)*

- Exercise Director for US Army Europe Foreign Consequence Management exercises, which test the ability of US Army Europe and US European Command to respond to foreign chemical, biological, radiological and nuclear incidents, in coordination with the US Department of State and host nation ministries of interior and indigenous consequence management forces. *(Building Coalitions)*

- Spearheaded US Army Reserve (USAR) Schools Initiative in US Army Europe, increasing interoperability by teaching US military doctrine to foreign military partners and the US interagency. *(Results Driven)*

Major General, US Army Reserve   01/2002 - 05/2005
Deputy Director Planning, Washington, DC   Hours per week: 40
Supervisor: Jerry Winters; 555.497.4488; Contact: Yes

Advised Director, Strategic Plans in support of Chairman, Joint Chiefs of Staff top calendar issues for defense plans and programs. Served as Host Team Leader for Chemical Weapons Convention Challenge Inspections and annual challenge inspection exercises. Expert at annual NATO Crisis Management exercise. Represented the Organization and top leadership at international conferences, Joint Staff Talks, and other events.

Key Leadership Initiatives:
- Senior US military representative at US Department of State-led conferences and negotiations: Organization for Security and Cooperation in Europe, Proliferation Security Initiative, and EUCOM-sponsored conference for the Economic Union Of West African States. At Proliferation Security Initiative conference, participated in negotiations with Russian contingent to achieve tangible commitments to this critical undertaking. *(Building Coalitions)*

- Conducted diplomatic negotiations gaining respect of allied hosts. Directly contributed to Mexico's decision to begin Joint Staff Talks; led the annual Joint Staff Talks with Chile. *(Building Coalitions)*

Brigadier General, US Army Reserve   07/1995 - 01/2002
3rd Army Reserve Command, Germany   Hours per week: 40
Supervisor: Andrew K. Myers; 202.555.2002; Contact: Yes

Led a major subordinate organization of United States Army Europe, composed of 34 units and 2,000 Reserve and Active-duty Soldiers, and civilian employees. Full accountability for ensuring subordinate units were manned, properly trained, and maintained a high rate of readiness for mobilization. Administered, planned, and executed an operating budget of $30M. Recommended and instituted a routine mobilization preparedness regimen, and associated issuing guidance, for all units including enhanced measures in response to 9/11 to ensure personnel and unit mobilization readiness across the organization.

Key Leadership Initiatives:

- Realigned force structure to meet the evolving needs of the total Army. Initiated an annual force structure review process with HQ US Army Europe (USAREUR) and its major subordinate commands. *(Leading Change)*

- Guided implementation of Equipment Storage Site-Expanded concept, producing a validated 97% equipment serviceability rate from previous 75%, in just one year. Outsourced logistics, increasing by 25% the time for units to focus precious training time on their core competency: mission operations. *(Results Driven)*

- Consolidated units into Reserve Centers, achieving greater return on investment in facilities and automation infrastructure, as well as synergies in administration and training. *(Leading Change/Results Driven)*

- Conducted negotiations with German Federal defense and finance ministries, gained HQ US Army Europe support, and achieved NATO "member of the force" status for the organization's drilling Reservists, thereby providing them the same PX and commissary access as Reserve Soldiers in the USA. *(Building Coalitions/Results Driven)*

EDUCATION & US ARMY PROFESSIONAL MILITARY EDUCATION

- **Master of Business Administration**, University of Maryland, 1998
- **Bachelor of Science in International Relations**, University of Virginia, 1987
- **National Security Management Course**, National Defense University, 1998
- **US Army Command and General Staff Officer Course**, 1997

PUBLIC SPEAKING ENGAGEMENTS

- "US Army Europe in Transformation." Delivered speech in German, 2011
- American Chamber of Commerce Serbia, and Serbian and international press. "Update on International Operations and Investments in Serbia," Serbia, 2009
- Press conference, UN Palace of Nations, Geneva, Switzerland, 2008

Conferences / Symposia

- Annual Serbia and Albania Economist Intelligence Unit conferences, 2000 - present
- First Annual Proliferation Security Initiative Conference, Warsaw, Poland, 2009

OTHER

Languages: German 3/3 • French 3/3

Military Awards & Decorations:

- Legion of Merit
- Defense Meritorious Service Medal
- Meritorious Service Medal
- Army Commendation Medal
- Army Achievement Medal

Clearance: TS/SCI

Sample Short Accomplishment Bullets for Your Resume

Below are shortened versions of the ECQ samples found in Chapter 5 starting on page 82. See how we shortened the longer versions and highlighted the important aspects of the accomplishment.

Leading Change

The same Leading Change stories from Chapter 5 are shown below edited down to shorter versions as mini-leadership stories, with evidence of the required ECQ leadership competencies identified from OPM, which can be used as bullets within a five-page SES resume-based application.

When short leadership bullets are integrated into the five-page resume, some information under scope of responsibilities/duties will already be addressed in the resume in the job description/ duties overview for each position (e.g., oversight leadership as Chief Information Officer [CIO] for Delta's worldwide technology management with 1,900 people and $350M in planned expenditures within the IT Division). Consequently, that information does not need to be included in the mini-leadership story bullets.

Short Leading Change Bullets

Delta Air Lines Turnaround Story (~75 words / 490 characters with spaces)

- I spearheaded the design of a long-term strategy/operational plan that would stretch corporate view to a three-year horizon by addressing short- and long-term planning, effectively forecasting all expenditures, and creating value for stakeholders. Winning approval from executive councils, the new planning process was embraced as a critical element of the Company's planning regimen. Capital spending dropped by 25% allowing for an increase in the capital spending program, reaching $1.5B.

Economic Transformation in Iraq (~125 words / 855 characters)

- Challenged to focus on the strategic objective of improving the Iraqi economy, I faced numerous obstacles to affect major organizational changes, in an environment of violence and fluidity: making changes to operational focus, creating capacity in the organization to take on increased work, developing common processes, and introducing infrastructure changes across the enterprise. I led the organization's shift in primary focus and completely revamped my organization's role in the region—I began supporting nation building; addressing NATO issues, growing infrastructure, designating economic safe zones, and building trust amongst the Iraqi business people and public. I led my organization in delivering a wider range of services, with much broader impact—at the national level, and transformed a tactical operation into a strategic powerhouse.

Leading People

The same Leading People samples from Chapter 5 are edited down to the shorter versions below as mini-leadership stories, with evidence of the required ECQ leadership competencies identified from OPM, which can be used as bullets within a five-page SES resume-based application.

Every effort was made to ensure that the conflict management and diversity competencies were addressed in the shorter versions.

Short Leading People Bullets

Employee Buy-In for Performance Improvement (~ 75 words / 535 characters with spaces)

- To turn around an underperforming team with the lowest customer satisfaction ratings ever, and put a critical program on track, I had to gain employee "buy-in." I designed employee engagement forums to share my vision, and led discussions seeking ideas for change, commitment, and opportunities to promote inclusion. I applied sensitivity in addressing past performance, and addressed conflict early. My leadership resulted in timely completion of projects, tripling of customer satisfaction ratings, and recognition by other managers.

Low Team Morale (~ 100 words / 720 characters with spaces)

- Empowered a diverse HQ staff with low morale; gained trust and energized a very talented management team and their direct-reports to exceed their potential. The management team handled their direct-reports in a very hierarchical, depreciative manner, resulting in many complaints and personnel turbulence. To establish the new leadership team, I scheduled an off-site meeting. I directed that the meeting be prepared and conducted by the new leadership team, who presented their proposals to senior management. This successful meeting institutionalized the new leadership construct and I achieved an enduring transformation to a leadership culture of inclusion, empowerment, and teamwork. The Region showed markedly improved morale and reduced personnel turbulence.

Results Driven

The same Results Driven samples from Chpater 5 are edited down to shorter versions below as mini-leadership stories, with evidence of the required ECQ leadership competencies identified from OPM, which can be used as bullets within a five-page SES resume-based application.

Every effort was made to ensure that results were clearly addressed and presented with an organizational, wide-reaching impact.

Short Results Driven Bullets

Created a New Organizational Structure for Agency (~100 words / 685 characters with spaces)

- Initiated an Agency-wide review of the organizational structure of the Agency; designed a politically sensitive strategy and transformed the entire organizational structure resulting in a drastic reduction of EEO complaints (from 11 to one), the elevation of numerous positions to appropriate grade levels, and a future plan for reducing incorrectly classified grade levels. Employees were briefed on the changes to win support. I crafted a communication plan for Congress explaining the new changes. The organizational structure and strategy I proposed was approved by the Agency, the Senate and House Appropriations Committees, and the EEO and HR Divisions, and was implemented in FY10.

Created Profitable Operations (~118 words / 739 characters with spaces)

- I turned around a business that had been hemorrhaging cash for the previous two years. Despite the company's purchase of two plants with capacity to fulfill more than 20% of market demand, the business had not been properly developed. Facing a "start-up" situation, I developed a strategy to address the personnel and business issues, aligned the organization behind key business processes focused on the development of the domestic market, and initiated a hiring and sales training program. I had set the conditions for a robust domestic sales and distribution organization. Within six months, the company doubled its sales volume with domestic sales—a company record, and the company showed a profit for the first time in three years.

Business Acumen

The same Business Acumen samples from Chapter 5 are edited down to the shorter versions below as mini-leadership examples, with evidence of the required ECQ leadership competencies identified from OPM, which can be used as bullets within a five-page SES resume-based application.

All three prongs of Business Acumen are addressed in these stories: Financial Management, Human Capital Management, and Technology Management.

Short Business Acumen Bullets

Secured Location for National Center (~ 90 words / 640 characters with spaces)

- I championed the planning and construction of a joint-use public-private facility dedicated to simulation and training, public safety, and forensic science for a University-hosted National Center for Forensic Science. Funding was not available for office space or a facility, so I envisioned a state-funded facility on federal land (no-cost lease) in exchange for office space for federal employees. I gained approvals from Congress, State of Florida, University, DoD, DOJ, Navy Facilities and Engineering Command, Research Park authorities, local regulatory bodies, and others; and approval for state appropriations for construction costs.

NSPS (~100 words / 695 characters with spaces)

- I designed human capital strategies to meet organizational mission and goals, and focused a Process Action Team (PAT) in establishing performance and developmental expectations, policy, and procedures to fully implement the National Security Personnel System (NSPS) for the Naval Audit Service (1,200 personnel). The team also developed an automated system designed as a program management tool. I guided my team to successfully meet the due date, and management approved the performance plans, procedures, business rules, and tools. We achieved our Strategic Objective of effectively and efficiently implementing the NSPS performance-based plan. All 1,200 auditors attended all NSPS training.

Building Coalitions

The same Building Coalitions samples from Chapter 5 are edited down to the shorter versions below as mini-leadership examples, with evidence of the required ECQ leadership competencies identified from OPM, which can be used as bullets within a five-page SES resume-based application.

Every effort was made to ensure that results focused on far-reaching coalition building and partnerships for mutual interests.

Short Building Coalitions Bullets

Missile Defense Coalitions (~65 words / 450 characters with spaces)
- I built a solid coalition between the National Reconnaissance Office (NRO) and the Missile Defense Agency, which is expanding to other Intelligence Community (IC) organizations. I drafted and staffed an overarching Memorandum of Agreement (MOA), which was ultimately signed by the Director NRO and Director MDA in 2010. That MOA serves as the keystone document for myriad engagements and formal [funded] projects between these two organizations.

Audit Coalition (~140 words / 865 characters with spaces)
- I led two multi-location overseas audits, while reviewing the Department of Army's checks and balances intended to detect, deter, and prevent fraud, waste, and abuse in contracting operations outside the USA. To lead this audit, I had to coordinate and develop relationships with Senior Leadership officials from 12 different DoD and Department of Army organizations worldwide. This audit was conducted in Africa and the other team was in Bahrain. All 12 DoD and Army disbursing and contracting Command Activities concurred with the 19 audit recommendations and took immediate action to improve the operations. All six Flag Officers recommended to the Auditor General of the Army the establishment of an audit office in Italy to provide audit coverage for the entire Europe, Africa, and Asia regions. Led completion of the audit in 150 days, 49% less time than normal.

Technical Qualification Samples

The samples below are shortened versions from TQ samples found in Chapter 5 starting on page 101. These bullets can be added to the five-page SES federal resume.

1. Experience in formulating, developing, implementing, and revising policies, strategies, and processes for national security programs related to natural or other disasters and emergency response (~105 words / 810 characters)

- I spearheaded the transformation of the organization's emergency response apparatus from a traditional, locally focused, disaster control element, to a nationally oriented emergency management machine. I merged Air Force, state and local emergency response agencies into one powerful emergency management operation, capable of managing multiple events, while effectively coordinating response actions with many internal and external stakeholders. I established an Air Force Incident Management System (AFIMS)-compliant Emergency Operations Center (EOC) 33% ahead of schedule. For actual and follow-on simulated emergency situations, I reduced the response time needed to establish multi-event command and control by approximately 15-30 minutes, a significant improvement in this time-sensitive environment.

2. Experience in developing and implementing organization-wide operations and processes for deployment, security, and oversight of large scale technology services, and leading broad cultural change in information technology management roles (~130 words / 905 characters)

- Designed the strategy and executed the Law Enforcement Information Sharing Program (LEISP) focused on changing the culture of law enforcement information sharing from "need to know" to "need to share," to systematically improve the investigation and prosecution of criminal activity. Persuaded numerous Agency law enforcement components to support the LEISP. Focused the reallocation of resources to design a data distribution facility to support the publishing and distribution of 100 million records. I guided the dramatic expansion of shareable law enforcement data from 22 million records to 60 million records, and an increase in state and local partnerships from six to more than 32, enabling 2,900 federal, state, local, and tribal law enforcement agencies to enter into productive nationwide information sharing partnerships across the broader federal law enforcement and intelligence community.

3. Experience in developing and implementing organization-wide operations and processes for advanced engineering and manufacturing operations and addressing specific needs or challenges (~70 words / 500 characters)

- I championed and led an Enterprise Resource Planning (ERP) upgrade to meet Sarbanes-Oxley compliance for the corporation and transformed three separate operational structures into one, joining the corporation under one Product Engineering (R&D) Division. All departments adopted and implemented the newly written policies and procedures. During an inspection, only three months after implementation, the entire corporation met and exceeded inspection requirements—a first ever for the corporation.

Excerpt from a successful ECQ

ECQ: Business Acumen
Negotiated First Joint-Use Public-Private Facility for National Center

"As a Department of Defense Senior Program Manager, championed the planning and construction of a joint-use public-private facility dedicated to simulation and training, public safety, and forensic science for a University-hosted National Center for Forensic Science. Funding was not available for office space or a facility. I envisioned a state-funded facility on federal land (no-cost lease) in exchange for office space for federal employees. I gained approvals from Congress, State of Florida, University, DOD, DOJ, Navy Facilities and Engineering Command, Research Park authorities, local regulatory bodies, and others; and approval for state appropriations for construction costs."

Read the one-page CCAR version of this Business Acumen ECQ starting on page 93.

Chapter Seven

Lessons Learned

Top Writing Tips Gleaned from the Qualifications Review Board's Disapproval Letters and from Expert SES Writers

When an application has been reviewed by the QRB and disapproved for SES certification, the QRB responds with a letter containing recommendations for improvements to be made to the ECQs. A candidate is then usually offered an opportunity to revise the written documents and return them to the QRB for a second review.

From our years of experience in working with SES-aspiring clients, we have had the opportunity to see the most common mistakes made by applicants. We have also reviewed OPM guidance on best practices for writing SES applications. Follow the tips below to put your absolute best foot forward in writing your executive federal resume and ECQs.

Writing Tip #1: Write effectively and clearly.

Each ECQ should be assessed for relevance, clarity, detail, objectiveness, and effectiveness.

The written documents submitted to an agency and the Qualifications Review Board must persuasively demonstrate decision-making and leadership abilities, indicating evidence of the 28 leadership competencies required of OPM. Write in an active voice at an executive level. Articulate specific examples and avoid use of vague descriptions. Responses should convey actions and clearly describe the difference that your leadership created within an organization.

Spell out acronyms, avoid jargon, and describe ranks and terms that may be misunderstood. A member of the QRB many not be familiar with your functional area of expertise or even your agency/company. Do not assume the readers will understand your position, even when using what might be considered standard acronyms.

Avoid passive construction or bureaucratic phrasing:
- A passive sentence structure may read: Responsible for; tasked with...
- An active sentence structure may read: I decided; I directed; I led...

Avoid generalities or vague references:
- *Vague:* I manage a staff of 18 supporting policy development.
- *Clarify:* I lead an office with 18 senior interagency personnel detailed from six different agencies. Guide staff in policy development and planning to improve the sharing and dissemination of information across the government for national security.

Writing Tip #2: Translate acronyms, jargon, and ranks.

Acronyms: Always spell out acronyms in the first instance. For example, PMA could be an acronym for: President's Management Agenda, Promotion Marketing Association, or Project Management Association. EVP (Executive Vice President) and CIO (Chief Information Officer) may seem commonplace, but they need to be spelled out in the first entry within each document.

Jargon: Jargon is specialized language relating to a specific activity, profession, group, or event. For example, "Commander 9th Army Reserve Command (9th ARCOM)" could be translated to CEO or Executive Officer of an organization based in Europe with 7,000 people in 14 different locations dispersed throughout four countries.

Military Ranks: Be mindful when using military rank or acronyms. For example, a Captain in the Army is a junior officer; a Captain in the Navy is a senior officer. Be sure to describe the appropriate scope of leadership when using military ranks and other terms.

Tip: Use the Readability Statics function in Microsoft Word to determine characters/word lengths, percentage of passive sentences, and the reading grade level.

Lessons learned from disapproval letters:

- Spell out acronyms, even common ones such as CIO.
- Make sure your narratives are not jargon-heavy.
- Do not use "i.e." or "e.g." Instead, use "that is" or "for example," respectively.

Writing Tip #3. Write stories that are relevant and recent; avoid opinions, beliefs, and philosophies.

The government seeks executives who are ready to lead in today's ever-changing environment and current with legislation and activities happening in Congress. Use recent examples focusing on the past three to five years, when possible, and expand to no more than 10 years. Additionally, the QRB is focused on what you have done as a manager and leader, so your examples need to cover your "hands-on" experience and focus on accomplishments. Use "I" statements, instead of "we" statements, taking full credit for leading organizations to produce results.

Lessons learned from disapproval letters:

- Do not use stories more than 10 years old.
- Use "I" statements—take ownership of your accomplishments.
- Change all the "we" entries to "I" entries. Change "We..." to "I led my staff..."
- Remove personal philosophy from your narrative. Avoid "in my opinion."
- Do not include negative comments about a particular group.

Writing Tip #4. Follow the CCAR (Challenge, Context, Action, Result) model.

OPM's recommended format for writing the Executive Core Qualifications is CCAR, to ensure all elements of each story are clear to the reader. The QRB members look for evidence of the CCAR format within the context of the essays and within the five-page resume-based application. It is easy to make laundry lists of duties and accomplishments, but the lists need to be drafted into CCAR essay stories that flow and are easy to read and understand.

Lessons learned from disapproval letters:

- Use ALL of the CCAR components for each story when possible.
- Present a clear picture of the substantive challenges and context rather than a list of duties.
- Make your CCAR components easy to identify.
- Strengthen your results.

Writing Tip #5. Be specific and illustrate results with qualitative and quantitative examples.

Use precise numbers to describe budgets, personnel, dates (timeframe), and other factors. Avoid use of "various," "numerous," or "several"—these are terms that make people guess. Convey enough familiarity with the results and the methods by which they were achieved, to ensure the reader understands the full context of the environment and the achievement.

As you write your accomplishment and results, make a comparison between the organization/ situation before you led change and after you achieved the change.

Lessons learned from disapproval letters:

- Use dollar amounts, percentages, and numbers in your results.
- Make your results as strong and clear as possible.
- Instead of, "Finally..." write, "This resulted in..." This makes the results easy for the reader to identify.
- Write-ups for Leading Change and Leading People are often too narrow in scope. Address changes you made to the entire organization and the impact of those changes on the organization.

Writing Tip #6. Write about leadership.

Your ECQs must demonstrate effective application of what you know as an executive leader. The ECQs should not merely describe personal growth, but rather describe the difference that you made that reached and influenced other people, other organizations, and policies.

Write about major accomplishments, not about how you developed skills. Many of the KSA (knowledge, skills, and abilities) statements written for General Schedule positions are effective when candidates demonstrate progressive responsibility, increasingly complex skill sets, or movement up the career ladder. However, the SES selects candidates who can demonstrate, through their leadership and management accomplishments, that they are capable of leading an organization now.

Review each ECQ to see how your example:
- reflects innovation
- describes your talent
- matches other examples
- amplifies your explanation of the challenges you faced
- presents the specifics of your solutions
- explores what distinguishes you
- uses objective instead of subjective descriptors

Lessons learned from disapproval letters:

Leading Change

- Show evidence of strategic thinking or vision.
- Include specific actions of how you led change.
- Describe the transformation that occurred. Show how it went beyond just an improvement of current processes.
- Demonstrate how you led change at the executive level.
- Write about any changes you caused to happen outside your organization.

Tip: Ask the following questions to help define how you led change:

- Is the organizational vision evident?
- Did I transcend vision into action?
- Is it evident that I strategically initiated and implemented transformational change?

Leading People

- Show how you pulled together a team, motivated them, and personally influenced the outcome despite challenges.
- Talk about instances where you leveraged diversity or managed conflict.
- Give examples of how you created an environment that affords independence and efficient action in order to meet the organization's needs.

Tip: Ask the following questions to help define how you led people:

- What is the largest staff I led; what were the challenges in leading this large staff?
- How did I lead the team through a challenge?
- How did I deal with conflicts that arose within the team?

Results Driven

- Make your results very clear.
- Focus on what the organization accomplished with you in charge.

Tip: Ask the following questions to help define how you delivered results:

- How did the priorities and objectives I set lead to high quality/quantity results?
- How did I address the needs of stakeholders and customers (internal and external)?
- How did I identify problems and implement solutions that resulted in improved services?

Business Acumen

- Include solid evidence of actual financial and human capital management.
- Discuss your human capital management experience (defined as building and managing workforces based on organizational goals, budget considerations, and staffing needs;

ensuring employees are appropriately recruited, selected, appraised, and rewarded; taking actions to address performance problems). Don't blend with Leading People competencies.

- Technology management should include online and multi-media staff training and use of social media.

Tip: Ask the following questions to help define how you demonstrated business acumen:

- What is my experience in creating and administering budgets and resources? Is it evident?
- What is my experience with a multi-sector workforce? What percentage of backlog was eliminated or reduced?
- How did I utilize technology to create or improve programs? What difficulties did I address in integrating this technology?

Building Coalitions

- Explain how you brought groups together or developed relationships between two or more organizations.
- Demonstrate that you not only organized groups, but led them as well.

Tip: Ask the following questions to help define how you built coalitions:

- What groups/networks (internal and external) did I partner with to achieve goals?
- How did I bring groups together? What challenges did I face?
- How did I build alliances and gain help and support to accomplish organizational goals?

Writing Tip #7. Cite recent education and training.

Include continual education that enhances skills in particular factors (for example, to address the cross-cutting fundamental leadership competency: "Continual Learning"). If education or training is included, it needs to be specific, executive level, and recent (SES development training that was completed within a recent five-year window is relevant).

Here are some examples of recent, targeted education and advanced professional development:

- Graduate of the Reid Buckley School of Public Speaking and the Karrass Seminar for Effective Negotiating
- Master of Arts/Strategic Communication and Leadership, Seton Hall University
- Defense Information School Public Affairs Officer Qualification Course, Advanced Distributed Learning, Resident (12 months)
- Senior Executive Service Developmental Training, USDA Graduate School, Washington, DC

Writing Tip #8. Proofread and edit all written documents.

Believe it or not, the QRB will actually point out your typos in a disapproval letter. Draftsmanship and executive writing are critical to a well-prepared SES application package. Executive writing includes understanding your audience and the purpose of the documents; writing effectively, clearly and concisely; using active voice; using leadership terms (for example, instead of, "I assisted the agency head," write, "I advised the agency head"); and developing stories that are persuasive with a strategic message that delivers results. What you say matters to the readers; impart a compelling message and the strength of your leadership qualifications. OPM is expecting a professional and polished document. Proofread and edit all written documents more than once and ask a friend, family member, or colleague to also proofread your written documents. Print out your document and proof on paper, not just on the computer. If time affords, let your document sit for a day before you proof. Read it aloud to check flow.

Use spell check, but do not reply on it. For example, "manger" is a perfectly good word that will not be flagged as a misspelling in the spell check function, and without a thorough proofreading, "manger" may replace "manager" in the document.

Tip: Draft all written documents in a Word file, and then copy and paste or transfer the information to online builders. Do not draft resumes and ECQs in online builders, as you have greater opportunity to make typographical and grammatical errors, and, in some cases, you may not be able to retrieve what you wrote. You always want to keep a record of your submission.

Lessons learned from disapproval letters:

- Avoid typos like "contacting resources" (should be "contracting resources") that spell check will not catch.
- Check for missing words, such as "neglected the opportunity [to] improve operations".
- Make sure what you wrote makes sense.

Writing Tip #9. Follow the "How to Apply" instructions perfectly.

Analyze the submission requirements carefully to ensure that you are submitting the required documentation, which may be a five-page resume-based application, or an executive federal resume and set of ECQs and TQs (the announcement may specify if the narratives can be one or two pages or a certain character length). Some announcements also request copies of transcripts, an SF-50 (federal personnel action), references, writing samples, or other requirements. Candidates may be disqualified for not submitting a complete package.

ECQ: Results Driven
Turned Mismanagement Into Efficiency, As Directed By Congress

"As Director of Workforce Planning I initiated an Agency-wide review of the organizational structure of the Agency. Designed a politically sensitive strategy and transformed the entire organizational structure resulting in a drastic reduction of EEO complaints (from 11 to one), the elevation of numerous positions to appropriate grade levels, and a future plan for reducing incorrectly classified grade levels. Employees were briefed of the changes to win support. I crafted a communication plan for Congress explaining the new changes. The organizational structure and strategy I proposed was approved by the Agency, the Senate and House Appropriations Committees, the EEO and HR Divisions, and implemented in FY10."

Read the one-page CCAR version of this Results Driven ECQ starting on page 90.

Chapter Eight

The Structured Interview

A structured interview is one in which all candidates are asked the same questions by an interview panel, in the same order, and in more or less the same way. Of course, interviews have long been an essential method for deciding whether a candidate is a "good fit" for a given position. But the structured interview takes this technique to the next level by giving each applicant an equal chance to respond and then scoring those responses systematically so that candidates can be compared objectively.

Structured interviews are becoming an important part of the SES application process for a couple of reasons. First, OPM requires agencies to perform structured interviews based on the Executive Core Qualifications when using the resume-based selection process described above. In the absence of the usual narrative statements addressing the ECQs, agencies would otherwise not have enough information to make a valid selection. In effect, the interview fills the gap left by missing ECQ statements by providing another way to obtain the same information, the only difference being that the responses are oral, not written.

Some of the federal agencies still using the traditional format applications are also starting to incorporate a structured interview into their SES selection process. They believe they learn important things about the applicant that they would never learn from written statements or a less rigorous "informal" interview. The bottom line, then, is that the SES job applicant today needs to be prepared to describe his or her ECQs effectively in an interview setting, regardless of the application method used for the particular job.

Behavior-Based Questions

A structured interview often includes behavior-based questions. SES applicants must understand that the major underlying factor in the use of the structured interview is found in the axiom, "Recent past performance is the best predictor of future performance." Behavior-based questions ask about a candidate's past performance, which is an indicator of similar future performance. Behavioral questions ask, "What have you done?" as opposed to, "What would you do?" Evaluators asking behavior-based questions want to hear how a candidate managed a program, not how the candidate would manage a program if presented with the opportunity.

The interviewers are looking for CCAR-type responses—stories of how a candidate led a program and directly affected organizational change with tangible results. Most structured interviews include a set number of questions within a set timeframe; consequently, candidates need to respond succinctly to questions providing enough context to help the interviewer understand the scope and breadth of the situation; describe the challenges to help the interviewer understand the complexity; describe actions taken to resolve the issue; and describe results—individual results and organizational results.

Behavior-based response to the question, "Describe your ability to manage large funds":

> "As the CIO for my Agency, I accounted for, justified, and administered a $200 million budget before Congress. Specifically, I developed a proposal to justify additional funding of $50 million to ensure IT requirements for warfighters in combat. These systems included smart phones, delivering up-to-the-minute data searches for Soldiers in warzones who, for example, might encounter a new type of IED. Due to budget cuts and freezes, I developed a communications plan and my senior staff met personally with all members of the appropriations committee. It took more than one year, but I successfully obtained the plus up funds, and a plan is in motion now to design and deliver high-level technology to warfighters.

The above response follows the CCAR format and clearly describes the candidate's mastery of his ability to manage large funds and obtain funding to support his programs.

A non-behavior-based response would begin like this: "If I were a manager of funds, I would develop proposals to justify why I would need additional funding to support major programs..."

During the interview process, and even in the application packages, avoid the use of opinions, philosophies, and "How you would do it if you were hired" responses. Phrases to avoid include, "I believe", "I feel", "I think"—these are opinion statements.

What to Expect During a Structured Interview

- The selecting official or designate will do a "read in" that establishes the parameters and expectations of the interview (i.e., time allowed, number of questions, taking notes, holding your questions to the end, and other items).

- Often, the interviewers will ask the candidate, "Tell us a little about yourself," followed by: "What makes you a good applicant for this position?"

- They will then take turns asking questions that have you "describe" your experience in the CCAR format.

- If you leave out any of the CCAR components, they may follow up with a probing question, seeking more information and a more detailed description of that specific component.

- The panel, when done, will ask if you have any questions about the position or agency.

- The interview will close, and the interviewers will thank you for your participation.

A Step-by-Step Approach to Preparing for an SES Behavior-Based Interview

The critical interview preparation steps listed below are based on a curriculum taught at federal agencies throughout the United States to prepare employees for better interview performance. Applicants who completed these steps frequently reported that they were well-prepared, confident, and felt like they "knew the job" as a result.

Step 1: Analyze the Job Announcement Line by Line
Locate the announcement for the position for which you'll be interviewing, or any other job description you've been provided, and analyze each sentence in the Duties section and the TQs of the SES announcement. Be sure to save any announcement for which you apply!

Step 2: Prepare Your Content
Your responses to behavior-based questions are essentially the same as the CCAR stories you developed for your ECQs and accomplishment bullets. Review these stories to prepare yourself for a behavior-based interview. Make sure that you have written at least five stories to prepare for your interview, using examples that are related to the criteria you have analyzed in the job announcement. Then turn each of your ECQ stories into seven or eight talking points that make it easier to practice and memorize your stories. It is important to practice speaking your interview stories so that you will be fluent in and easily remember your best examples.

In the interview, talk about these examples with animation and enthusiasm to demonstrate your past performance in a positive way. Point out how your leadership strategies and skills helped you to succeed.

Step 3: Study OPM's Practical Guide to Structured Interviews
OPM's guide to structured interviews can be found at http://apps.opm.gov/ADT/ContentFiles/SIGuide09.08.08.pdf.

Many SES interviews are structured interviews, meaning that the interviewers are trained, the questions are determined in advance (based on the leadership competencies), and each candidate is asked the same questions. A structured interview is used so that it can be objective, enabling the interviewer to score each answer and compare the performance or response of one candidate to that of another.

Step 4: Research the Agency and Office to Learn the Latest Leadership News and Challenges
Research the agency and office carefully. Print pages from their websites. Find and memorize their mission. Discover who their customers are. Try to research any new challenges or changes occurring in the office or agency.

Step 5: Plan and Practice
Don't cut corners! Take the time to prepare properly by following these guidelines:

- Remember that nothing will make you look worse than not knowing what you put on your own resume. Study your resume carefully and be able to speak about it knowledgably.

- Prepare an executive level one-minute response to the "Tell me about yourself" question.

- Prepare three reasons why they should hire you. Memorize these.

- Write at least five success stories to answer behavioral interview questions.

- Prepare three questions for you to ask the interviewer.

- Practice with a tape recorder or video camera if you can. Listen to your voice. Watch your body language. If recording is not an option, consider practicing in front of a mirror or with a friend or colleague who can offer constructive feedback.

Step 6: Be Confident That You Are a Leader
Here are tips to consider before the interview:

- As you prepare to leave for the interview, make sure to take a printed copy of your reference list, paper and pen for note taking, and directions to the interview site. You could also take your last Strategic Plan or other important document that demonstrates your successful leadership in case it will help you to show it to the interview panel.

- Arrive 10 to 15 minutes early for your interview.

- Stand and greet your interviewer(s) with a firm handshake.

- During the interview, be conscious of your body language and eye contact. Crossed arms make you appear defensive, fidgeting may be construed as nervousness, and lack of eye contact may be interpreted as being untrustworthy. Instead, nod while listening to show that you are attentive and alert. Most importantly, do not slouch.

- If you are in a panel interview, keep your eyes moving from person to person slowly. Show that you are engaged with each person.

- Think before you answer and have a clear understanding of the question—if you don't, ask for clarification.

- Express yourself clearly and convey confidence but not over-confidence.

- Adjust your response length based on the number of questions you will be asked. If you are in an hour-long interview and you will respond to five questions, then adjust your responses to about five to eight minutes per response—that provides time for the panel to ask follow-up/probing questions, and time for you to ask questions of the panel at the conclusion of the interview. If the panel will be asking seven questions, then adjust your responses to three to five minutes each. Gauge your time as you move through the interview. If the panelists look bored, yawn, or fidget, cut your example short and move to the results.

- Show a sincere interest in the organization and position.

- Focus on what you can contribute to the organization rather than what the employer can do for you.

- Do not place blame on or be negative about past employers.

- End the interview on a confident note, indicating that you feel you are a good fit for the position at hand and can make a contribution. Emphasize your interest in the position and what you can bring to the organization.

- Thank the interviewer(s) and ask for a business card so that you will have the necessary contact information for follow-up.

- After the interview, promptly and carefully write gracious letters to thank the interviewers for their time and to remind them of the valuable qualifications you bring to the job. Don't miss this last chance to market yourself and highlight your skills relevant to the position!

Preparing Your CCAR Examples

Use the worksheets on the following pages to prepare interview responses for each of the ECQs. You may have already done this for your written ECQs or accomplishment bullets, but going through the process again will help you remember the details for the interview.

Interview Preparation Sheet: Leading Change

Creativity and Innovation | External Awareness | Flexibility | Resilience | Strategic Thinking | Vision

Interview Story Title:

Challenge:

Context:

Action:

Result:

Interview Preparation Sheet: Leading People

Conflict Management | Leveraging Diversity | Developing Others | Team Building

Interview Story Title:

Challenge:

Context:

Action:

Result:

Interview Preparation Sheet: Results Driven

Accountability | Customer Service | Decisiveness | Entrepreneurship | Problem Solving | Technical Credibility

Interview Story Title:

Challenge:

Context:

Action:

Result:

Interview Preparation Sheet: Business Acumen

Financial Management | Human Capital Management | Technology Management

Interview Story Title:

Challenge:

Context:

Action:

Result:

Interview Preparation Sheet: Building Coalitions

Partnering | Political Savvy | Influencing/Negotiating

Interview Story Title:

Challenge:

Context:

Action:

Result:

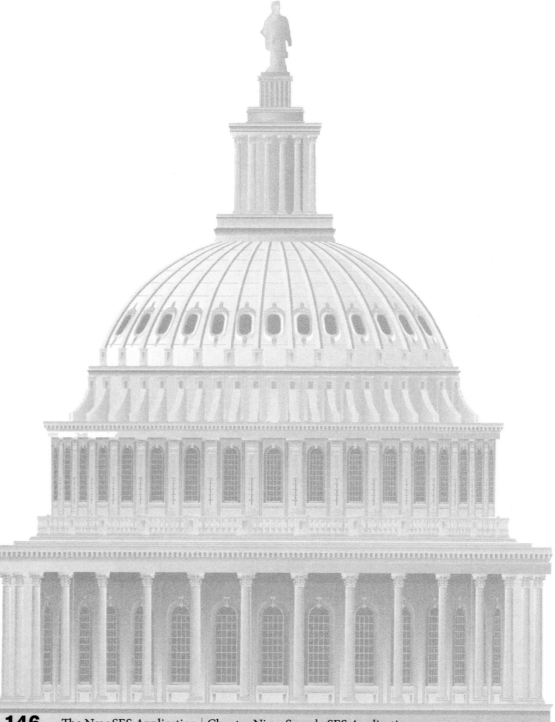

Chapter Nine

Sample SES Applications

Table of Contents

Case Study 1 – International Corporate Executive/Military Officer

Target Agency and Position: Executive Director, Mobilization & Training, Department Of Navy

Judy Johnson (name fictionalized) had an exciting and interesting parallel industry and military Reserve career for more than 20 years. She was a senior executive for a consumer goods corporation, and a military officer for the Reserve Component in Europe. When she decided to apply for an SES position, we transformed her Resumix into a senior-level federal resume package with full ECQ essays and a five-page SES resume.

Judy submitted her application against fierce competition. The Agency received approximately 117 applications for this coveted position, a position that would support the Agency's Secretary. Of the 117 applications, eight candidates were interviewed by a panel, in a structured interview environment with behavior-based questions. Of the eight who were interviewed, two were selected to interview with the Agency head. Judy was selected for the position and her ECQs were certified by the QRB.

Our focus was on highlighting her executive leadership across a diversity of organizations and describing powerful accomplishments, concentrating on the position description and Technical Qualifications. Keywords are in bold:

- Knowledge in **directing the development and implementation of new policies** for **Reserve readiness and training**

- Ability to **initiate programs, actions**, and **ensure adherence** to established **policies** and **national security objectives**

- Ability to **develop systems** and **standards** for the **administration of approved plans** and **programs**

- **Advisor to Agency head** and other senior stakeholders for **readiness, training, and operations, policy guidance, and program direction**

- Participate in **conducting analyses, providing guidance, making recommendations**, and **issuing guidance** for **defense plans and programs**

JUDY JOHNSON

Permanent: Judy@gmail.com
5420 Constantine Avenue   Cell: 555.202.4986
Washington, DC 92865
Announcement Number: SES-2011, Executive Director, Mobilization & Training, Dept. of Navy

INDUSTRY EXPERIENCE

Executive Vice President, USA Region   **10/2009 - present**
Consumer Goods USA, Long Beach, CA

Implemented a strategic vision for business operations and development in the USA region of this international company with offices in 20 countries. Supervise large staff of 200+ including a sales force and plant workers, and independent distributors across five countries. Manage cross-cultural issues, enforce EEO regulations, and create programs to heighten morale and foster diversity. Manage a budget worth $7.9M.

Vice President, Corporate Marketing Initiatives, 06/2005 - 10/2009

Corporate-wide single point of contact for regulatory compliance and initiatives. Developed and implemented Direct Marketing vision, strategies, programs and budgets. Supervised 100+ staff and administered $47M marketing budget. Articulated instructions for Annual & Strategic Plan HQ instructions.

Accomplishments:
- Actively managed the Compliance Working Group in creating strategic and contingency plans for corporate response to regulatory trends. Ensured that financial and commercial impacts of directives were incorporated into Headquarters and individual market operating and strategic plans.
- Achieved the on-time, on-budget implementation of a corporate-wide consumer products directive. Compliance with the directive was named a corporate priority for the upcoming three-year period, as the out-year's corporate budget planning was already underway, and thus would have visibility with the Board of Directors.
- Heightened corporate acceptance of inevitable increased future regulation.
- Led implementation of corporate-wide Internet-based direct marketing pilot program.

Vice President, Imports, 12/2003 - 06/2005

Reported to Regional President as member of Regional Executive Committee. Supervised staff of 28. Managed all aspects of importation of sales of high-margin brands into the USA.

Accomplishments:
- Successfully disengaged from importers, thwarting importer strategy of multi-million dollar cash extraction and disturbance of commercial operations.

General Manager, Consumer Products USA, 1998 - 2003

Responsible for $100M in domestic sales, distribution and marketing of products manufactured in two local factories, plus export sales to other countries.

Military

Major General, US Army Reserve, 05/2005 - Present
Deputy Chief of Staff, Headquarters

Principal advisor to Commanding General, US Army Europe on all reserve component affairs and activities. Monitor processes for training and readiness of the Reserve component. Liaison between Commanding General, US Army Europe and Chief, Army Reserve and Director, Army National Guard for development of plans, policies and procedures for coordination and synchronization of Reserve Component integration into US Army Europe peacetime training support, as well as contingency operations.

US Army Reserve Component, 01/2002 - 05/2005
Major General, US Army Reserve

Assisted Director, Strategic Plans in support of Chairman, Joint Chiefs of Staff top calendar issues. Served as Host Team Leader for Chemical Weapons Convention Challenge Inspections and annual challenge inspection exercises. Expert at annual NATO Crisis Management exercise. Represented the Office at international conferences, Joint Staff Talks, and other events.

Brigadier General, US Army Reserve, 07/1995 - 01/2002
Commanding General, 3rd Army Reserve Command
Germany

Led a major subordinate command of United States Army Europe, comprised of 34 units and 2,000 Reserve and Active-duty Soldiers, and civilian employees. Full accountability for ensuring subordinate units were manned, properly trained, and maintained a high rate of readiness for mobilization. Administered, planned, and executed an operating budget of ~$10M. Instituted a routine mobilization preparedness regimen for all units including enhanced measures in response to 9/11 to ensure personnel and unit mobilization readiness.

EDUCATION
*   Master of Business Administration, University of Maryland, 1998
*   Bachelor of Science in International Relations, University of Virginia, 1987
*   National Security Management Course, National Defense University, 1998
*   US Army Command and General Staff Officer Course, 1997

We worked with Judy to develop a list of top ten major career accomplishments and leadership initiatives, focused on the ECQs and TQs from the announcement. From this list, we drafted full ECQ essays. (We did not draft CCAR stories for Judy in the below examples, as we did for Keith.) To finalize the package, we wove short summary versions of the ECQ essays into the five-page SES resume. Here is the top ten list, describing Judy's diverse career:

1.   Improved morale with new leadership team (Leading People)

Led a diverse headquarters' staff in Long Beach composed of personnel from two US regions, the Headquarters, and members from two countries. This comprised the management team and the mid-level staff. The management team handled their direct-reports in a very hierarchical, depreciative manner, resulting in many complaints and personnel turbulence. Under my guidance, I introduced team-building requirements and the staff showed markedly improved morale and reduced personnel turbulence.

2.   Analyzed trends among regions and led change to incorporate 10-year assessment of trends (Leading Change)

Developed, agreed upon, and implemented a strategic vision for Consumer Goods USA's business operations across the nation and the plants in 20 other countries to standardize operations reflecting 5- to 10-year assessment of regional trends including Free Trade Agreements; market regulatory trends; trade evolution; and competitive strategies. Incorporated relevant elements into annual and strategic business objectives, plans, programs and budgets, including organizational and business mode shifts.

3.   Led Regulatory Compliance Group (Business Acumen)

Actively managed the Regulatory Compliance Working Group in creating strategic and contingency plans for corporate response to regulatory trends. Ensured that financial and commercial impacts of directives were incorporated into Headquarters and individual market operating and strategic plans.

4.   Business turnaround after hemorrhaging cash (Business Acumen)

Turned around a business unit that had been hemorrhaging cash for previous two years. Rallied organization behind vision statement. Closed two plants. Controlled imports of high-margin premium brands.

5.   Oversaw two major Joint Army and Air Force Exercises, Special Operations Forces (Leading People)

Oversaw two major Army and Air Force exercises. Led a multi-service staff team and multiple Army and Marine organizations in planning and execution as part of a US-led Joint Task Force operating in a sovereign host nation. Determined the forces required for both combat and post-combat phases; set the theater for port, airfield and basing needs; coordinated flow in and staging of forces and materiel.

6.   Exercise Director, Foreign Consequence Management Exercises (Building Coalitions)

Exercise Director and principal advisor for US Army Europe Foreign Consequence Management exercises, which tested the ability of US Army Europe and US European Command to respond to foreign chemical, biological, radiological and nuclear incidents, in coordination with the US Department of State and host nation ministries of interior and indigenous consequence management forces.

7.   USAR Schools Initiative (Results Driven)

Spearheaded US Army Reserve (USAR) Schools Initiative in Europe, increasing interoperability by teaching US military doctrine to foreign military partners and the US interagency.

8.   Selected as Deputy Chief of Staff, Operations for several months (Results Driven)

Oversight leadership for 1,200 Soldiers and civilians and 21 divisions, supporting war plans, training, exercises and international operations for 70,000 Soldiers in US Army Europe; as well as the deployment and redeployment of US Army Europe units and individuals to Iraq and Afghanistan for Operations Enduring Freedom and Iraqi Freedom.

9.   Consolidated units into Reserve Centers (Results Driven)

Achieved greater return on investment in facilities and automation infrastructure, as well as synergies in administration and training.

10.   Principal advisor to Commanding General, US Army Europe (Technical Qualification & Building Coalitions)

Advisor to senior leadership for all Reserve Component affairs, activities, and policy development in region. Monitor processes for training and readiness; serve as liaison between numerous stakeholder organizations for the development of plans, policies, and procedures for coordination and synchronization of Reserve Component integration into US Army Europe peacetime training support, as well as contingency operations.

The executive federal resume may be used in an online federal resume builder (like USAJOBS) or as a hard copy / uploaded resume in a Word document (per the vacancy announcement). The online version should be in the OUTLINE format as seen here, to help the reader identify key leadership competencies and technical qualifications required from the vacancy announcement. The hard copy version, at about three to five pages, does not need to be in the outline format. It provides the same profile information and same functional category headers, with shorter accomplishment bullets than the five-page resume-based application. The short accomplishment bullets will be more fully addressed in the CCAR format in the ECQ and TQ essays that accompany the executive federal resume.

JUDY JOHNSON
5420 Constantine Avenue
Washington, DC 92865
Day Phone: 555.202.4986
Email: Judy@gmail.com

WORK EXPERIENCE **Consumer Goods USA** **10/2009 - Present**
Long Beach, CA

Salary: 150,000 USD Per Year
Hours per week: 60

EXECUTIVE VICE PRESIDENT

Consumer Goods USA is a consumer goods business with 25,000 employees in 20 countries across the globe.

OVERSIGHT LEADERSHIP FOR IMPLEMENTING A STRATEGIC VISION for business development and operations in the USA region of this international company. Supervise 65 office staff, 80 field sales personnel, and provide dotted-line supervision to 175 plant workers and independent distributors across five countries. Manage an operational budget worth $7.9M. Incorporate relevant elements into annual and strategic business objectives, plans, programs and budgets, including organizational and business mode shifts.

PERSONNEL ADMINISTRATION: Manage cross-cultural issues, enforce EEO regulations, and create programs to heighten morale and foster diversity. Empowered and coached staff with low morale, gained trust, and energized a very talented management team and their direct-reports to exceed their potential.

KEY ACCOMPLISHMENTS:

ACQUISITION MANAGEMENT: Integrated the brands, employees, distributors, and business operations of a major company acquisition in 2009.

BUSINESS DEVELOPMENT: Achieved annual and strategic plan (3-year planning horizon) volume and profit targets.

FACTORY INTEGRATION: Ensured full integration of new plant in Long Beach. Melded marketing and sales organization from east coast for office support (Finance, IT, Logistics, Legal & HR) and ensured cooperation between HQ marketing and sales departments, HQ R&D and Global Supply Chain.

(Contact Supervisor: Yes, Supervisor's Name: Tom Hansen, Supervisor's Phone: 555-349-2940)

US Army Europe   **5/2005 - Present**
The Pentagon & Germany
                       Salary: $25,000 USD Per Year
                       Hours per week: 30

DEPUTY CHIEF OF STAFF (MAJOR GENERAL), HEADQUARTERS

PRINCIPAL ADVISOR TO COMMANDING GENERAL, US Army Europe on all Reserve Component affairs and activities. Monitor processes for training and readiness of the Reserve Component. Liaison between multiple military components for development of plans, policies, and procedures for training support and contingency operations. Oversight leadership for 1,200 Soldiers and civilians and 21 divisions. Organizational representative at meetings, events, and exercises. Unique additional leadership oversight includes:

KEY ACCOMPLISHMENTS:

OPERATIONS MANAGEMENT: Led two major Army and Air Force exercises. Supervised and guided a multi-service staff team and multiple Army and Marine organizations in planning and execution as part of a US-led Joint Task Force operating in a sovereign host nation.

EXECUTIVE MENTORSHIP: Appointed Deputy Exercise Director for the next Fiscal Year's major exercise, which entails mentoring an active component Major General (senior officer) and leading the ground force activities of the Joint Exercise Control Group.

TRAINING PROGRAM: Spearheaded US Army Reserve (USAR) Schools Initiative in Europe, increasing interoperability by teaching US military doctrine to foreign military partners.

Consumer Goods USA **6/2005 - 10/2009**
Cincinnati, OH   **Salary: $140,000 USD Per Year**
                        Hours per week: 40

VICE PRESIDENT, CORPORATE MARKETING INITIATIVES

CORPORATE-WIDE SINGLE POINT OF CONTACT for regulatory compliance and initiatives. Developed and implemented Direct Marketing vision, strategies, programs and budgets. Supervisor of 100+ staff. Administered $47M marketing budget. Articulated Regulatory market instructions for Annual & Strategic Plan HQ instructions.

KEY ACCOMPLISHMENTS:

COALITION BUILDING: Actively managed the Regulatory Compliance Working Group in creating strategic and contingency plans for corporate response to regulatory trends.

PROGRAM MANAGEMENT: Guided development of and achieved the

on-time, on-budget implementation of a corporate-wide consumer products directive, which saved the company $45 million over five years.

TECHNOLOGY INTEGRATION: Led implementation of corporate-wide Internet-based direct marketing pilot program. (Contact Supervisor: Yes, Supervisor's Name: Donald Andersen, Supervisor's Phone: 49.555.874.9230)

Consumer Goods USA	**12/2003 - 6/2005**
Long Beach, CA	**Salary: $105,000 USD Per Year**
	Hours per week: 40

VICE PRESIDENT, IMPORTS

OVERSIGHT SUPERVISION FOR SENIOR STAFF of 28. Directed multi-functional team of operations in five countries. Managed all aspects of importation of $70M sales of high-margin premium and sub-premium brands. Reported to Regional President as member of Regional Executive Committee.

KEY ACCOMPLISHMENTS:

NEGOTIATIONS: Successfully negotiated and managed disengagement from importers, thwarting importer strategy of multi-million dollar cash extraction and disturbance of commercial operations.

PROJECT MANAGEMENT: Managed full project management lifecycle of multi-functional operations team for plant R&D, HQ Packaging, and marketing & sales staff to ensure synchronized Product, Packaging, Operations Planning, Marketing and Selling activities.

INTERNATIONAL FINANCE: Secured return of bank guarantees of $28 million via successful negotiations with customs authorities.

(Contact Supervisor: Yes, Supervisor's Name: James Smith, Supervisor's Phone: 555.349.7811)

US Army Reserve Component	**1/2002 - 5/2005**
Washington, DC US	
	Salary: $25,000 USD Per Year
	Hours per week: 40

DEPUTY DIRECTOR PLANNING, MAJOR GENERAL, US ARMY RESERVE

ASSISTED DIRECTOR, STRATEGIC PLANS IN SUPPORT OF CHAIRMAN, JOINT CHIEFS of Staff top calendar issues. Expert at annual NATO Crisis Management exercise. Represented the Office at international conferences, Joint Staff Talks, and other events.

KEY ACCOMPLISHMENTS:

COMMUNICATIONS: Senior US military representative at US Department of State-led conferences and negotiations. At Proliferation Security Initiative conference, participated in negotiations with foreign contingent to achieve tangible commitments to this critical undertaking.

JOINT NEGOTIATIONS: Guided diplomatic negotiations gaining respect of allied hosts. Directly contributed to Mexico's decision to begin Joint Staff Talks; led the annual Joint Staff Talks with Chile.

PROCEDURES DEVELOPMENT: Developed first-ever Host Team Leader brief delineating Host Team activities that were synchronized with pre-established inspection timelines. This brief was incorporated into Host Team standard procedures.

(Contact Supervisor: Yes, Supervisor's Name: Jerry Winters, Supervisor's Phone: 555.497.4488)

Commanding General,   **7/1995 - 1/2002**
3rd Army Reserve Command
Europe, Germany

Salary: $25,000 USD Per Year
Hours per week: 40

BRIGADIER GENERAL, US ARMY RESERVE

LED A MAJOR SUBORDINATE COMMAND of United States Army Europe, composed of 34 units and 2,000 Reserve and Active-duty Soldiers, and civilian employees. Administered and executed an operating budget of ~$30M. Supervised 15 direct-report subordinate managers.

OPERATIONS MANAGEMENT: Fully accountable for ensuring subordinate units were manned, trained, and maintained a high rate of readiness for mobilization.

KEY ACCOMPLISHMENTS:

PROCEDURES DEVELOPMENT: Realigned force structure to meet the evolving needs of the total Army. Initiated an annual force structure review process with HQ and its major subordinate commands.

PROGRAM DEVELOPMENT AND LEADERSHIP: Instituted a routine mobilization preparedness regimen for all units including enhanced measures in response to 9/11 to ensure personnel and unit mobilization readiness.

EQUIPMENT MANAGEMENT: IMPLEMENTED EQUIPMENT STORAGE SITE-EXPANDED CONCEPT, producing a validated 97% equipment serviceability rate from previous 75%, in just one year.

LOGISTICS MANAGEMENT: Outsourced logistics, increasing by 25% the time for units to focus precious training time on their core competency: mission operations.

(Contact Supervisor: Yes, Supervisor's Name: Andrew K. Myers, Supervisor's Phone: 202.555.2002)

EDUCATION   University of Maryland
College Park, MD US
Master's Degree - 5/1998
Major: Masters in Business Administration

University of Virginia
Charlottesville, VA US
Bachelor's Degree - 6/1987
Major: International Relations

National Defense University
Washington, DC US
Some College Coursework Completed, 1998
Major: National Security Management Course

PROFESSIONAL PUBLICATIONS

PUBLIC SPEAKING ENGAGEMENTS AND WRITTEN PRESENTATIONS:

- "US Army Europe in Transformation". Delivered speech in German, 2011
- American Chamber of Commerce Serbia, and Serbian and international press. "Update on International Operations and Investments in Serbia", Serbia, 2009
- Press conference, UN Palace of Nations, Geneva, Switzerland, 2008

Conferences / Symposia
- Annual Serbia and Albania Economist Intelligence Unit conferences, 2000 - present
- First Annual Proliferation Security Initiative Conference, Warsaw, Poland, 2009

ADDITIONAL INFORMATION

EXECUTIVE PROFILE

- 20-year Corporate Career / Senior Sales & Marketing Executive / Consumer Goods USA
- Major General, US Army Reserve (1989 - present)
- Multi-lingual: German & French
- TS/SCI

Senior executive with full oversight direction for strategic planning and business leadership for large, geographically separated organizations, hundreds of employees and multi-million dollar operating budgets, while holding dual careers with multi-national, fast-moving consumer goods corporations, and in leading US Army organizations. Develop policy and regulatory compliance. Culturally acclimatized, politically correct, and diplomatic; excellent political-military skills. Structure joint operations.

The paper version of Judy Johnson's federal executive resume for the traditional SES application can be found in Chapter 5 starting on page 107. This version is a simple re-formatting of the USAJOBS resume on the previous pages in order to look better when printed on paper.

FIVE-PAGE SES FEDERAL RESUME

To draft Judy's five-page SES federal resume, we took her paper version executive federal resume (shown on the previous pages) and pulled the short CCAR accomplishment bullets, ensuring that all ECQs, TQs, keywords, and other skills and competencies were addressed in the resume.

You can find Judy's five-page SES federal resume starting on page 116 in Chapter 6. The ECQs are identified in the sample in italics for your convenience, but the labels would be removed before submission.

JUDY JOHNSON

Permanent:
5420 Constantine Avenue, Washington, DC 92865

Judy@gmail.com
Cell: 555.202.4986

Date

Susan Smith, HR Director
Dept. of Navy Mobilization & Training
The Pentagon, Washington, DC 22210

Announcement Number: SES-2011, Executive Director, Mobilization & Training, Department of Navy

Dear Ms. Smith and Executive Review Panel:

Enclosed is my five-page SES resume-based application, with the ECQs and TQs addressed within the body of the resume, for the position of Executive Director, Mobilization & Training, Dept. of Navy.

I offer a rare blend of senior leadership from within industry and from serving as an officer for the US Army Reserve. My policy and military regulatory compliance development, financial management, personnel administration and management of large workforces around the globe, and corporate experience, complemented by broad operational skills in mobilization, deployment, training, readiness, and logistics and top-tier client relationship management, is a solid fit with the Executive Director position.

Throughout my career, I have proven my ability in building productive teams, applying a direct communication style, advising senior leaders and stakeholders, and making recommendations and issuing guidance for defense plans and programs, as well as building sustainable programs delivering replicable results for industry.

As the representative of my organization at international conferences, I am comfortable speaking to all echelons and responding to questions concerning training and mobilization of forces overseas, serving as a subject matter expert and authority. I excel at policy development and implementation, and negotiating challenging issues with foreign nationals delivering positive results. Additionally, as a military officer, I seek to continue to support the military through this government position.

If these qualities and experiences might enhance your organizational mission, I will be pleased to make myself available for an interview to describe my capabilities as a senior leader and how I can benefit your agency with my credentials. Thank you for your consideration.

Sincerely,

Judy Johnson

Enclosure: Resume

Case Study 2 – Audit Director (Keith Smith)

Target Agency and Position: Executive Director, Auditing Services, Defense Contract Audit Agency

Keith Smith (name fictionalized) worked with the Department of Defense (in two different agencies) as an auditor for 20 years, successfully moving up the federal ladder reaching the GS-15 level, and was often tapped to serve in an acting Director role for major audits. During his career, he led highly complex audits that saved the DoD up to $900 million. With specialized experience in leading multi-billion dollar audits across the globe, he is also the recipient of major and notable awards.

We developed a top ten list of accomplishments, drafted full CCAR ECQ essays, and then prepared the five-page SES federal resume using short accomplishment bullets (summarized from the longer CCAR ECQ essays). We illustrated his expertise by focusing on the position duties, the technical qualifications, and the 28 SES leadership competencies required for the position. The full package also included an executive cover letter depicting his interest in the position and an overview of his qualifications as a good fit for the position.

The SES resume that we wrote demonstrated that he met the leadership competencies to be referred, interviewed, and selected for an SES position in the agency he targeted; and his ECQs passed the Qualifications Review Board. The final resume includes the keywords identified in bold:

- Knowledge of applicable **laws** and **auditing standards**
- Ability to **manage large auditing or accounting programs** and **organizational elements** with strong emphasis on **policy development**
- Superior knowledge of **advanced fraud auditing techniques**
- Ability to **lead efficient planning and execution** of the **financial management audit program**
- **Delegate** responsibility and authority for program execution to **key staff** and **monitor accomplishment**
- **Collaborate** with the **most senior level military and government** officials to discuss risks and audit progress. Ability to **develop and lead high level working groups**
- **Public speaking**

KEITH SMITH

6916 Thunder Hill Street
Columbia, MD 20853
Announcement Number: SES-1010 / Executive Director, Auditing Services

202.654.5555
keithsmith@gmail.com

PROFESSIONAL EXPERIENCE

DEPARTMENT OF DEFENSE, 1987 - PRESENT

Audit Director (YC-3 GS-0511 / GS-15 equivalent), 11/2004 - Present
Department of Army, Washington, DC

- Oversee the activities of 1,000 professional auditors, to include Defense Contract Management Agency, Army Systems Command Earned Value Management Technical Experts, and Defense Contract Agency Audit auditors, divided among five audit teams.
- Supervise a direct-report leadership staff.
- Pointed the way for major financial management control changes to the program and financial management reviews of all DoD major acquisition programs.
- Report directly to the Assistant Auditor General of the Army for Research, Development, and Acquisition Audits.

Supervisory Auditor (GS-0511-15), 09/2000 - 11/2004
Department of Army, Washington, DC

- Responsible for 39 Audit Service auditors to include Systems Command Earned Value Management Technical Experts and Defense Contract Agency Audit Auditors conducting 3,000 audits annually.
- Supervised my staff's planning and simultaneous execution of single and multi-location audit projects involving multimillion-dollar DoD weapon systems acquisition programs geographically dispersed worldwide.
- Briefed and interacted with senior leaders.
- Drafted and established office policy and the staffing structure needed to accomplish the assigned audits.

Program Executive Auditor Advisor, 05/1997 - 09/2000

- Competitively selected to serve as Program Executive Officer (PEO) Auditor to two different Acquisition Commands.
- Program Executive Officer for Air Antisubmarine, Assault, and Special Mission Programs Office; and Air Systems Command, to re-engineer the acquisition auditing process.
- Ensured continuous real-time acquisition auditing, management, and leadership guidance to 42 major program offices executing 300 acquisition programs to nail down achievement of program cost, schedule, and performance objectives.
- Responsible for over 100 modifications and upgrades involving the 300 acquisition programs.

Team Leader, Supervisory Auditor, GS-511-13, 1992 - 1997

- Managed the full range of audit responsibilities for complex areas of weapon systems acquisition and operational audits in the Capitol Region.

EDUCATION

- MBA, University of Maryland
- BS in Accounting, University of Maryland
- Defense Leadership and Management Program (DLAMP), DOD, Washington, DC
- Senior Executive Service Developmental Training, USDA Graduate School, 2007
- The Federal Executive Institute, Leadership for Democratic Society, 2006
- Defense Acquisition University, Department of Defense Acquisition Program Management Office Course, 2003
- Department of the Army Civilian Financial Management Career Program, 1998

CERTIFICATIONS

Certified Acquisition Auditor Level III
Defense Acquisition Workforce Improvement Act Level I, Program Management
Contracting Officer Representative

SPEAKING & PUBLICATIONS

Speaker, Defense Audit Agency Training Conference addressing the series of Earned Value Management audits within the Department of Army and Department of Defense, 2011

Speaker at the first annual United States Africa Command Contracting Workshop, 2009

Co-Author, "Earned Value Management, Is It Working?" The Management Control Program Herald, an Assistant Secretary of the Army for Financial Management Publication, 2006

PERFORMANCE AWARDS

Society of Military Comptroller's Meritorious Performance Award for Auditing
Special Act Award
Auditor of the Year

To organize Keith's accomplishments, we developed his top ten list of accomplishments within the past 10 years and included a short detail or result for each accomplishment:

1. Acting Assistant Auditor General

Routinely appointed as the Acting Assistant Auditor General for Research, Development, Acquisition, and Logistics Directorate, a Senior Executive Service (SES) level position, with executive management for 60 professional auditors. Brief the Secretary of the Army, the Under Secretary of the Army, the Assistant Secretary of the Army for Research, Development and Acquisition, the Assistant Secretary of the Army for Financial Management and Comptroller, and numerous Flag Officers, Secretariat-level, and other Senior Executives.

2. Transformed Earned Value Management in DoD

Transformed use of Earned Value Management (EVM) within DoD and Department of Army (DA). Led audit to determine what changes were needed to reinvigorate the EVM program and use it effectively across all DoD acquisition programs to achieve its strategic goal of providing affordable weapon systems to Sailors and Marines. The result was use of EVM in DoD and with DoD contractors, ensuring program offices properly used EVM as a management tool and Soldiers and Sailors received affordable, timely weapon systems.

3. Developed new DoD-wide policies to support launch of Joint Training Program for Defense Acquisition Contractor University

Developed and implemented new DoD-wide policies and formed a new DoD working group composed of senior members from all DoD agencies to ascertain priority and proper use of EVM, establish and launch a joint training program at the Defense Acquisition Contractor University, and create a DoD EVM Center to retrain the workforce and implement the policies to control costs for weapons development.

4. Trained 600 auditors and eliminated time for training

Introduced a training program for 600 auditors within the Audit Service to eliminate the time that program personnel spent educating auditors, to dismantle barriers, and to cultivate better relationships between the internal audit and acquisition communities. This program resulted in enhancing the Audit Service's credibility within the acquisition communities, increased our client focus and responsiveness, and expanded our inventory of products and services to meet client needs.

5. Guided two major overseas audits – Africa and Bahrain

Guided the planning and execution of two overseas audits, while reviewing the Department of Army's checks and balances intended to detect, deter, and prevent fraud, waste, and abuse in contracting operations outside the USA. Received full approval for establishment of an audit office in Italy. Led completion of the audit in an accelerated 150 days.

6.   Reengineered acquisition audit process at six major Army Acquisition Commands

Spearheaded a reengineering effort of the acquisition auditing process at six major Army Acquisition Commands. My efforts resulted in the acquisition reform initiative changing how the DA Acquisition community views the Army Audit Service. This acquisition reform initiative moved the Program Executive Office to the forefront of implementation of innovative programs.

7.   Published three important audit reports

Published three audit reports with full agreement with the audit findings and recommendations resulting in:

a. DoD organizational changes related to financial management infrastructure, accountability for assets and operations, the reliability of financial information and compliance with public law, acquisition regulations; and

b. DoD terminating acquisition programs resulting in cost avoidance of $400 million and revising the Army acquisition policy regarding the financial management and oversight for acquisition programs.

8.   Improved morale, reduced conflict and increased productivity of audit team

Reversed internal conflict, poor morale and low productivity of an audit team, requested to conduct a politically sensitive audit for the Criminal Investigative Service, with DoD-wide implications. Introduced training and audit execution strategies, and refocused the audit on addressing the potential fraud issues.

9.   Led congressional audit of schedule slippage and contractor cost overruns

Led a high-visibility audit of an acquisition program that had experienced significant cost growth and schedule slippage, prompting intense Congressional scrutiny and oversight. Produced two high-impact and quick-reaction audit reports, six months ahead of schedule.

10.   Professional speaking

Speaker, Defense Audit Agency Training Conference addressing the series of Earned Value Management audits within the Department of Army and Department of Defense, 2011

Speaker at the first annual United States Africa Command Contracting Workshop, 2009

We expanded Keith's top ten accomplishments into short CCAR stories and identified each story with an appropriate ECQ for use in the five-page SES resume. For this example, we are only setting up five CCAR stories:

1. **Acting Assistant Auditor General (Leading People / TQ)**

   Challenge: I led strategic planning and execution of difficult and complex audits of multimillion-dollar Department of Army (DA) geographically dispersed weapon systems acquisition programs, navigating challenging agency and contractor resistance.

   Context: As the Audit Director, with oversight leadership for 1,000 professional auditors, I was routinely appointed as the Acting Assistant Auditor General for Research, Development, Acquisition, and Logistics Directorate, a Senior Executive Service (SES) level position, with executive management for 60 professional auditors divided among five audit teams.

   Action: I briefed the Secretary of the Army and numerous Flag Officers, Secretariat-level, and other Senior Executives on financial management issues concerning major defense acquisition programs.

   Result: Led my staff in producing numerous organizational improvements, resulting in the establishment of an Earned Value Management (EVM) Integrated Process Team, EVM Center of Excellence, and EVM policy and procedures changes.

2. **Transformed Earned Value Management in DoD (Leading Change)**

   Challenge: I faced furious opposition from the Government and contractor personnel regarding required changes for EVM.

   Context: Led a highly complex audit, requested by the Assistant Secretary of the Army.

   Action: Determined what changes were needed to reinvigorate the EVM program and use it effectively across all DoD acquisition programs to achieve its strategic goal of providing affordable weapon systems to Sailors and Marines.

   Result: Transformed use of Earned Value Management (EVM) within DoD and Department of Army (DA). The results of my change initiative transformed use of EVM in DoD and with DoD contractors, ensuring that program offices properly used EVM as a management tool, and that Soldiers and Sailors received affordable, timely weapon systems.

3. **Developed new DoD-wide policies to support launch of Joint Training Program for Defense Acquisition Contractor University (Leading Change)**

   Challenge: Developed a vision that required buy-in from many stakeholders.

   Context: Developed and implemented new DoD-wide policies.

   Action: Formed a new DoD working group composed of senior members from all DoD agencies to ascertain priority and proper use of EVM.

Result: Established and launched a joint training program at the Defense Acquisition Contractor University, and created a DoD EVM Center to retrain the workforce and implement the policies to control costs for weapons development.

4. **Trained 600 auditors and eliminated time for training (Business Acumen)**

Challenge: Needed to overcome the time that program personnel spent educating auditors, dismantle barriers, and cultivate better relationships between the internal audit and acquisition communities.

Context: Used education and introduced a training program for 600 auditors within the Audit Service.

Action: Developed a strategy to fully integrate myself as a member of the staff to execute this training program. Met with and shared my vision with the two Senior officials; met with their respective Program Managers.

Result: The auditing reform and additional training initiative enhanced the Audit Service's credibility within the acquisition communities, increased our client focus and responsiveness, and expanded our inventory of products and services to meet client needs; 90% percent of our acquisition audits are now addressing the Army's high risks area.

5. **Guided two major overseas audits – Africa and Bahrain (Building Coalitions)**

Challenge: Guided the planning and execution of two complex multi-location overseas audits, while reviewing the Department of Army's checks and balances intended to detect, deter, and prevent fraud, waste, and abuse in contracting operations outside the USA. There were serious conflicts among the groups as to what the report should address and the direction of recommendations.

Context: As the Audit Director, I led an audit to coordinate and develop relationships with Senior Leadership officials from 12 different Department of Defense and Department of Army Commands and Activities worldwide.

Action: Established a working group/coalition with the 12 DoD activities, and from this working group made recommendations.

Result: All six Flag Officers recommended to the Auditor General of the Army the establishment of an audit office in Italy to provide audit coverage for the entire Europe, Africa, and Asia regions. I led completion of the audit in an accelerated 150 days, 49% less time than normal.

After developing the CCAR essays, we then drafted the resume using the five-page resume-based format and pulled the story bullets into the resume, ensuring that all ECQs, TQs, keywords, and other skills and competencies were addressed in the resume. ECQs are identified here in the sample for your convenience, but the labels would be removed before submission.

KEITH SMITH

6916 Thunder Hill Street
Columbia, MD 20853

202.654.5555
keithsmith@gmail.com

Citizenship: U.S. Citizen

Social Security Number: xxx-xx-xxxx

Highest Federal Grade: GS-15

Announcement Number: SES-1010 / Executive Director, Auditing Services

EXECUTIVE PROFILE

Proactive senior leader with proven record of accomplishments leading internal audits across the Department of Defense (DoD) and with the Office of Inspector General, delivering cost effective audits to strengthen federal agencies and the DoD. Navigate and develop the annual audit plans, and submit audit topics addressing high-risk areas throughout large federal agencies. Create vision and focus for the development of clear and concise audit objectives, and first-ever audit programs for complex areas that lead to identifying significant audit findings.

Broad, deep strategic knowledge of Department of Defense military service specific programs spanning many functional areas including Research and Development, program and budget, support services, financial management, major systems acquisition, supply operations, contracting, and foreign military sales programs. Recommended Department of Defense-wide and federal agency-wide policy and program changes resulting in cost avoidance and savings of $900 million. Recognized for operational excellence; recipient of the Society of Military Comptroller's Meritorious Award for Auditing, for identifying $400 million in monetary benefits to the Department of Army.

PROFESSIONAL EXPERIENCE & SELECT ACCOMPLISHMENTS

DEPARTMENT OF DEFENSE, 1987 - PRESENT

Audit Director (YC-3 GS-0511 / GS-15 equivalent)
Department of Army, Washington, DC
Supervisor: Sherri Jones; 555.202.3861 (may be contacted)

11/2004 - Present
Hours: 40/Week

Oversee the activities of 1,000 professional auditors, to include Defense Contract Management Agency, Army Systems Command Earned Value Management Technical Experts, and Defense Contract Agency Audit auditors, divided among five audit teams; supervise a direct-report leadership staff and delegate authority for program execution. Pointed the way for major financial management control changes to the program and organizational elements, and financial management reviews of all DoD major acquisition programs. Report directly to the Assistant Auditor General of the Army for Research, Development, and Acquisition Audits.

Oversee strategic planning and execution of difficult and complex audits of multimillion-dollar Department of Army (DA) geographically dispersed weapon systems acquisition programs. Navigated through challenging agency and contractor resistance, and drove numerous organizational improvements, resulting in the establishment of an Earned Value Management (EVM) Integrated Process Team, EVM Center of Excellence, and EVM policy and procedures changes within the Department of the Army.

Leadership Accomplishments

- Routinely appointed as the Acting Assistant Auditor General for Research, Development, Acquisition, and Logistics Directorate, a Senior Executive Service (SES) level position, with executive management for 60 professional auditors. Brief the Secretary of the Army, the Under Secretary of the Army, the Assistant Secretary of Army for Research, Development and Acquisition, the Assistant Secretary of the Army for Financial Management and Comptroller and numerous Flag Officers, Secretariat-level, and other Senior Executives on financial management issues concerning a major defense acquisition programs. (Leading People)

- Transformed use of Earned Value Management (EVM) within DoD and Department of Army (DA). Led a large highly complex audit, requested by the Assistant Secretary of the Army, to determine what changes were needed to reinvigorate the EVM program and use it effectively across all DoD acquisition programs to achieve its strategic goal of providing affordable weapon systems to Sailors and Marines. Communicating my vision to reverse the problems and redirect the program, I guided Senior Acquisition leadership in assessing risks to improve efficiency, accountability, and program effectiveness. I then unveiled my audit strategy plan, and introduced a major shift in the method of conducting business with defense contractors; I led my teams into the offices of major defense contractors to evaluate the adequacy of their EVM systems against industry and DoD standards, a first-ever for the Army Audit Service. The results of my change initiative transformed use of EVM in DoD and with DoD contractors, ensuring program offices properly used EVM as a management tool and Soldiers and Sailors received affordable, timely weapon systems. (Leading Change)

- Spurred the development and implementation of new DoD-wide policies and formed and led a high-level DoD working group composed of senior members from all DoD agencies to ascertain priority and proper use of EVM, establish and launch a Joint training program at the Defense Acquisition Contractor University, and create a DoD EVM Center to retrain the workforce and implement the policies to control costs for weapons development. (Leading Change)

- Exploited education and introduced a training program for 600 auditors within the Audit Service to eliminate the time that program personnel spent educating auditors, to dismantle barriers, and to cultivate better relationships between the internal audit and acquisition communities. The auditing reform and additional training initiative enhanced the Audit Service's credibility within the acquisition communities, increased our client focus and responsiveness, and expanded our inventory of products and services to meet client needs; 90% percent of our acquisition audits are now addressing the Army's high risks area. (Business Acumen)

- Guided the planning and execution of two complex multi-location overseas audits, while reviewing the Department of Army's checks and balances intended to detect, deter, and prevent fraud, waste, and abuse in contracting operations outside the USA. To successfully lead this matrix and politically-sensitive audit, I formed collaborative working relationships with Senior Leadership officials from 12 different DoD and Department of Army organizations worldwide. This audit was conducted in Africa and the other team was in Bahrain. All 12 DoD and Army disbursing and contracting Command Activities concurred with the 19 audit recommendations and took immediate action to improve the operations. All six Flag Officers recommended to the Auditor General of the Army the establishment of an audit office in Italy to provide audit coverage for the entire Europe, Africa, and Asia regions. I led completion of the audit in an accelerated 150 days, 49% less time than normal. (Building Coalitions)

- Published and edited 12 audit reports with full agreement with the audit findings and recommendations resulting in DoD and DA organizational changes related to financial management infrastructure, accountability for assets and operations, and the reliability of financial information; and development of DA acquisition policy regarding the financial management and oversight for acquisition programs. (Results Driven)

Supervisory Auditor (GS-0511-15)
Department of Army, Washington, DC
Supervisor: John Jones; 202.555.5039 (may be contacted)

09/2000 - 11/2004
Hours: 40/Week

Oversaw and monitored the work of 39 Audit Service auditors to include Systems Command Earned Value Management Technical Experts and Defense Contract Agency Audit Auditors (GS-14/13/12) conducting 3,000 audits annually valued at $6.4 billion. Provided overarching management, delegation and leadership for my key staff's planning and simultaneous execution of single and multi-location audit projects involving multimillion-dollar DoD weapon systems acquisition programs geographically dispersed worldwide. Briefed and interacted with senior Department of Army leaders to include Senior Executives and Flag Officers. Drafted and established office policy and the staffing structure needed to accomplish the assigned audits.

Leadership Accomplishments

- Spearheaded a reengineering effort of the acquisition auditing process at six major Army Acquisition Commands within the Department of the Army (DA). Several studies on the oversight of the acquisition process had criticized internal auditors. Providing oversight guidance to 26 major program offices executing 119 acquisition programs, I ensured achievement of program cost, schedule, and performance objectives.

Efficiently planned an audit strategy to execute this reform initiative and shared my vision with the six Senior Acquisition officials and their respective Program Managers, remaining sensitive to the unique nature of this work, as it had not been done before. My efforts resulted in the acquisition reform initiative changing how the DA Acquisition community views the Army Audit Service. DA Senior Acquisition Leaders issued endorsement letters validating the success of this acquisition reform and their support for continuation. This acquisition reform initiative moved the Program Executive Office to the forefront of implementation of innovative programs. (Leading Change)

- Published three audit reports with full agreement with the audit findings and recommendations resulting in:

- DoD organizational changes related to financial management infrastructure, accountability for assets and operations, the reliability of financial information and compliance with public law, acquisition regulations; and

- DoD terminating acquisition programs resulting in cost avoidance of $400 million and revising the Army acquisition policy regarding the financial management and oversight for acquisition programs. Briefed the Secretary of Army on the results of the audit of Non-Acquisition Programs identifying $400 million in cost savings to the Department of Army. (Results Driven)

- Reversed internal conflict, poor morale and low productivity of an audit team, requested to conduct a politically sensitive audit for the Criminal Investigative Service, with DoD-wide implications. I took charge of the audit team, introduced training and audit execution strategies, and refocused the audit on addressing the potential fraud issues. I divided the group into teams with a focus on the specific areas addressing vulnerabilities and risks affecting the potential fraud indicators. These efforts greatly improved the team's level of expertise of specialized auditing functions, allowing the team to be responsive to leadership in managing a high-risk area by providing audit services of recognizable value. The audit team identified a security vulnerability involving contractor employees accessing restricted and controlled areas on Air Force, Army, Navy, and Marine Corps installations across the US. The report went to Chief of Army Operation Security Office and OSD Security Office; the Army took immediate action to address the risks affecting national security. Team members received special awards for outstanding performance. (Leading People)

- Led a high-visibility audit of an acquisition program that had experienced significant cost growth and schedule slippage, prompting intense Congressional scrutiny and oversight. The audit required intimate knowledge and expertise of Defense acquisition and contractors' accounting and financial management systems supporting the acquisition program. The assigned audit team lacked the requisite knowledge. Mentored and coached the new program manager and exposed the team to the requirements of the acquisition program by introducing advanced formal training. I obtained technical support from Subject Matter Technical Experts, to support our review of the contractors' accounting and management systems. Under my guidance, this audit team produced two high-impact and quick-reaction audit reports, six months ahead of schedule, on the acquisition program's failure to implement the required financial management controls to contain costs and schedules within the Agency's strategic objectives and goals for acquisition programs. (Leading People)

Program Executive Auditor Advisor (GS-511-14)   05/1997 - 09/2000
Department of Army, Washington, DC   Hours: 40/Week
Supervisor: Tom Linder; 555.210.4509 (may be contacted)

Competitively selected to serve as Program Executive Officer (PEO) Auditor to two different Acquisition Commands; Program Executive Officer for Air Antisubmarine, Assault, and Special Mission Programs Office; and Air Systems Command, to re-engineer the acquisition auditing process. Ensured continuous real-time acquisition auditing, management, and leadership guidance to 42 major program offices executing 300 acquisition programs to nail down achievement of program cost, schedule, and performance objectives. Guided more than 100 modifications and upgrades involving the 300 acquisition programs with annual budget of $5 billion.

Leadership Accomplishments

- Shared acquisition knowledge with 700 other auditors within the Audit Service resulting in the elimination of time program personnel spent educating auditors. (Business Acumen)

- Dismantled barriers and cultivated better relationships between the internal audit and acquisition communities, enhancing the Audit Service's credibility, increasing our client focus and responsiveness, and expanding our inventory of products and services to meet client needs. (Building Coalitions)

- Received a Letter of Appreciation from the Deputy Commander for Acquisition and Operation, a Senior Executive, for my contributions toward establishing the initial Integrated Program Team (IPT) Training Course. (Business Acumen)

Team Leader, Supervisory Auditor, GS-511-13, 1992 - 1997

Managed the full range of audit responsibilities for complex areas of weapon systems acquisition and operational audits in the Capitol Region.

EDUCATION

- MBA, University of Maryland, 1995
- BS in Accounting, University of Maryland, 1988
- Defense Leadership and Management Program (DLAMP), DoD, Wash., DC, 2009
- Senior Executive Service Developmental Training, USDA Graduate School, 2007
- The Federal Executive Institute, Leadership for Democratic Society, 2006
- Defense Acquisition University, Department of Defense Acquisition Program Management Office Course, 2003
- Department of the Army Civilian Financial Management Career Program, 1998

DEFENSE ACQUISITION RELATED CERTIFICATIONS

- Certified Acquisition Auditor Level III
- Defense Acquisition Workforce Improvement Act Level I, Program Management
- Contracting Officer Representative

PROFESSIONAL SPEAKING ENGAGEMENTS & PUBLICATIONS

- Speaker, Defense Audit Agency Training Conference addressing the series of Earned Value Management audits within the Department of Army and Dept. of Defense, 2011
- Speaker, 1st Annual United States Africa Command Contracting Workshop, 2009
- Co-Author, "Earned Value Management, Is It Working?" The Management Control Program Herald, an Assistant Secretary of the Army for Financial Management Publication, 2006

PERFORMANCE AWARDS

- Society of Military Comptroller's Meritorious Performance Award for Auditing
- Special Act Award
- Auditor of the Year

KEITH SMITH

6916 Thunder Hill Street
Columbia, MD 20853

202.654.5555
keithsmith@gmail.com

Date

Mr. John Smith
SES Recruitment Team
Defense Contract and Audit Agency
Alexandria, VA 22202

Re: Candidate for Executive Director, Auditing Services, DCAA Headquarters
       Announcement SES-1010

Dear Mr. Smith and DCAA Executive SES Recruiters:

Enclosed is my five-page SES Federal Resume, which addresses the ECQs and the Technical Qualifications within the body of the resume, for the position of Executive Director, Auditing Services, DCAA Headquarters.

Adept at leading internal audits across the Department of Defense (DoD) and with the Office of Inspector General with 20 years of experience, I guide my senior teams to deliver cost effective audits to strengthen federal agencies and the DoD. I bring to the table the financial and auditing management, negotiation skills, strategic planning, and relationship management skills imperative to conducting sensitive financial audits across the DoD worldwide.

As an advisor to the most senior leadership in our federal government and military, I offer expertise in Department of Defense and military service specific programs spanning many functional areas, including Research and Development, program and budget, support services, financial management, major systems acquisition, supply operations, contracting, and foreign military sales programs. Altogether as a DoD Audit Director, I have recommended Department of Defense-wide and federal agency-wide policy and program changes resulting in cost avoidance and savings of $900 million.

My professional leadership and technical expertise at department-level Audit Management will provide the direction required by DCAA to plan and execute Department of Defense audits and financial advisory services for all DoD Components.

Thank you for your consideration of my qualifications.

Sincerely,

Keith Smith

Enclosures: SES Federal Resume, SF-50

Index

About the Author
KATHRYN TROUTMAN

Kathryn Kraemer Troutman is the founder and president of The Resume Place, Inc., a service business located in Baltimore, MD, specializing in writing and designing professional federal and private-sector resumes, as well as coaching and education in the federal hiring process. For the past 30 years, Troutman has managed her professional writing and consulting practice, publishing and federal career training business, and with her team of 20 Certified Federal Resume Writers, The Resume Place advises and writes more than 300 federal resumes per month for military, private industry, and federal clients worldwide.

Internationally recognized as the "Federal Resume Guru" by federal jobseekers and federal human resources specialists, Troutman created the format and name for the new "federal resume" that became an accepted standard after the SF 171 form was eliminated in 1995. She is the pioneering designer of the federal resume based on her first book, the Federal Resume Guidebook, which already is in the fifth edition.

Troutman is an in-demand, government contract federal career trainer, who has trained thousands of federal employees in writing competitive federal fesumes, KSAs in the fesume, Senior Executive Service applications, and USAJOBS applications for more than 175 federal agencies in the United States and Europe. Her Federal Career Training courses and publications are listed on the GSA Schedule for government agency purchase. Her popular website, www.resume-place.com, receives more than 50,000 visitors per month, and provides online tools to assist with federal resume writing and federal job searches to jobseekers worldwide.

Troutman created the Certified Federal Job Search Trainer program—the first ever federal career train-the-trainer program for career counselors and military career counselors—using the popular curriculum, Ten Steps to a Federal Job, based on the award-winning book by the same name. Since 2002, more than 500 career counselors and workshop leaders have been licensed to teach the Ten Steps curriculum. In addition, the 62 U.S. Navy Fleet and Family Support Centers worldwide teach this curriculum to separating and retiring military personnel and family members as part of the Transition Assistance Program (TAP). U.S. Air Force, Coast Guard, and Army military transition centers use the Ten Steps Jobseeker Guide (workshop handout) and curriculum to help military personnel write federal resumes and submit to Resumix databases.

Some of Troutman's other federal career publications include the Federal Resume Guidebook, the award-winning Student's Federal Career Guide, and the Military to Federal Career Guide, which is used in every Navy and Marine Corps base and most Air Force career transition centers in the world.

Troutman is a Federal Career Coach to federal, military, and private sector jobseekers who are striving to achieve their first job in government or get promoted. She is a Certified Career Management Coach with specialized expertise in government careers and advises executives in achievement of Senior Executive Service ranks, as well as career management and growth for all career levels.

A frequent radio, TV, and online guest, Troutman answers questions about federal careers, resume writing, and job search techniques.

Diane Hudson Burns

Certified Federal Job Search Trainer & Counselor
SES Strategist, Writer & Trainer / SES Project Manager, The Resume Place
Certified Professional Resume Writer & Coach
Certified Leadership & Talent Management Coach
Federal Government Resumes & Application Procedures Specialist
Military Transition Authority

Diane Hudson Burns is a multi-credentialed career coach and executive resume writer and editor, specializing in posturing federal and non-federal employees to enter the federal government's Senior Executive Service (SES). She is an expert in writing SES and ECQ packages, coaching clients to define their strengths, and persuasively demonstrate writing their decision-making and leadership abilities, by "telling their leadership stories" according to the ECQ leadership competencies/requirements. She skillfully analyzes clients' core leadership qualifications and maps them to the ECQ competencies. Diane is an experienced trainer in Federal Resume, SES, ECQ/TQ, and KSA writing topics for SES Leadership Development program candidates at the Naval Ship Yard at Capitol Hill, and Air Force Leadership; for military employment readiness specialists and retiring military; as well as train-the-trainer at industry conferences internationally on outplacement and career search topics.

As an award winning resume writer, her achievements include "Best Executive Resume" award by the Professional Association of Resume Writers & Career Coaches. Her resumes, cover letters, and case studies are published in more than 60 books and periodicals; she is chapter author on military to civilian transition in the Federal Resume Guidebook, Third, Fourth, and Fifth Editions;

chapter author on the SES and the new five-page SES resume-based application in the Federal Resume Guidebook, Fifth Edition; and case study author for Ten Steps to a Federal Job, Second Edition. She writes columns and articles for numerous organizations and serves as the Veteran Expert for Job-Hunt.Org and as the Federal Expert for Workforce50.com.

Diane formerly held a federal job as a Special Agent Investigator for the Department of Defense, and was a Recruiter/Employment Specialist for a major aerospace corporation in Los Angeles, California. She holds a Bachelor of Science degree in Journalism from California State Polytechnic University, California, and a number of industry credentials. Diane is an active member of the Board of Directors, Professional Association of Resume Writers/Career Coaches (PARW/CC) and creator and Director of the Certified Professional Career Coach program; and an active member of the Career Management Alliance, as the monthly Federal Facts facilitator, and winner of the first annual Career Industry Mentor Award, 2010. She also serves as an outplacement coach for such organizations as CareerBuilder.

Diane has navigated four international moves, living abroad for 12 years and in the Washington, DC/Baltimore corridor for five years.

Paul Thompson

Paul Thompson is a management consultant based in the Washington, DC area. Mr. Thompson retired from federal service late in 2010 after a long and varied career at the U.S. Office of Personnel Management (OPM). Among has many positions at OPM, Mr. Thompson served on the evaluation team for the groundbreaking Navy ("China Lake") pay banding/pay-for-performance demonstration project and later managed demonstration project development, serving as OPM lead for both the NIST performance pay and USDA staffing demonstration projects. The USDA project pioneered the category ranking staffing system that has since become universal across the federal government. Mr. Thompson was also instrumental in developing the first framework for human resource management accountability, and later managed OPM's human capital outreach to several human and natural resource agencies. More recently, he managed Senior Executive Service (SES) policy for OPM, and led a project to establish a resume-based application process for potential SES members.

Mr. Thompson has written several reports and articles over his career, and was the primary author of the first Federal Human Capital Survey summary report in 2002. Since becoming a consultant he has worked with GSA and SIGTARP on SES performance management, and is a Strategic Advisor with the Partnership for Public Service. He is currently designing and implementing a performance management system for the National Labor Relations Board.

A native of Minnesota, Mr. Thompson is married and has two adult sons. He holds a B.A. from Carleton College, an M.A. from the University of Wisconsin - Madison, and an M.B.A. from the University of Maryland - College Park. He is an ardent amateur musician and also enjoys travel, baseball, theatre, and movies.

Get More Expert Help With Your SES Application!

The Resume Place Senior Executive Services Writers and Consultants are experts at preparing various formats that could be required by federal agencies. The total SES package is made up of the following application elements:

- Five-Page SES ECQ Federal Resume (NEW!)
- Executive Federal Resume
- Technical & Managerial Qualifications (one page each maximum or TQs might be included in your federal resume
- Executive Core Qualifications (ECQs) – Leading Change, Leading People, Results Driven, Business Acumen, and Building Coalitions/Communications
- Long-Form – Traditional ECQs: 8,000 characters, 10 pages maximum, past 10-15 years of experience, examples for each ECQ, CCAR format
- Short-Form – Leadership Competency ECQs: 5,000 characters, 5 pages max, past 15 years of experience, one long example or two short examples each in the CCAR format
- Executive Cover Letter

More Information:
www.resume-place.com/ses
(888) 480-8265

From the Foreword to the Federal Resume Guidebook, 5th Edition:

"So – what's the savvy job applicant to do? Clearly, they will need to do their homework and pay close attention to the relevant details about the job and the application process contained in the announcement for each federal job in which they are interested. Simply submitting the same boiler-plate resume and cover letter to every job one sees is not going to be nearly as successful as a carefully tailored response that speaks to the specifics of each job.

… **Kathryn Troutman** has literally made a career out of understanding and tracking the evolution of the federal hiring system and translating that understanding into practical advice for the job seeker."

John Palguta
Vice President of Policy
Partnership for Public Service

Free federal career info! >> *Visit www.resume-place.com/resources*

- Free webinars about federal resume and federal career consulting services
- Free webinars on Hiring Reform and how it will affect your federal job search
- Free KSA, Federal Resume, and Cover Letter Builders
- Up-to-the minute federal job search info—register for our informative newsletter
- Federal job search news articles, updated daily

Brought to you by:

Kathryn Troutman
Author, *Federal Resume Guidebook*
President and Founder of The Resume Place, Inc.
The Leading Federal Career Consulting and
Federal Resume Writing Firm in America

NEW! SES Application Writing Course

Join our expert and knowledgeable SES trainers for a two-day hands-on workshop in the Washington DC/Baltimore area and gain valuable instruction for senior federal managers and team leaders on writing, and developing quality written examples for the five mandatory ECQ essays for SES applications.

Participants will also learn how to package their extensive executive leadership and senior management experience into a concise and focused new 5-page SES ECQ Federal Resume with clear leadership accomplishments. Participants will also gain insight and effective tools for preparing Technical Qualifications and SES application Cover Letter.

Training location: **Federal Career Training Institute**, 79 Mellor Avenue, Catonsville, MD just minutes from Baltimore and the Capital Beltway.

This power-packed workshop covers:

- Writing the Senior Executive Service (SES) Executive Core Qualifications (ECQs)
- New Five-Page SES/ECQ Federal Application
- SES Interview Preparation
- This same two-day SES ECQ Writing Workshop has been held for AF, Navy, Army, EPA, NASA, DOI, and USMC leadership programs throughout the USA.

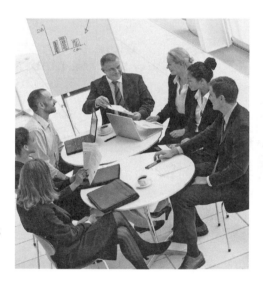

More information:
Email us at training@resume-place.com
or visit our website at www.resume-place.com/ses

Bring this course to your government agency office.
We are a GSA vendor / CCR registered / Small, Woman-Owned Business.

FEDERAL CAREER
Training Institute

Award-Winning, Best-Selling Career Books by Kathryn Troutman

FEDERAL RESUME GUIDEBOOK 5th Edition—Newly revised in 2011! Perfect for federal to federal jobseekers. This book is nearly 450 pages of comprehensive, in-depth guidance on how to craft the perfect federal application to change jobs or get promoted. The Federal Resume Guidebook is THE book that created today's federal resume.

TEN STEPS TO A FEDERAL JOB 3rd Edition—Just Released July 2011! Wouldn't it be great to have all the basic steps you need to land that dream federal job in just one book? *Ten Steps to a Federal Job* is that book, and with the 3rd edition, Kathryn Troutman outdid herself by adding new crucial details and background on the federal job search that you won't find anywhere else! Learn the tips and tricks to convert your private-industry resume into a winning federal format.

MILITARY TO FEDERAL CAREER GUIDE 2nd Edition—President Obama has created a new program to hire more vets into the federal government. But even if there are more jobs, applicants STILL have to write a competitive federal resume. This book is designed to help you translate military skills and competencies into the federal skills, keywords, and an outstanding resume.

JOBSEEKER'S GUIDE 4th Edition—The Jobseeker's Guide is the first-ever publication for military and family members who are seeking federal employment. This best-selling publication is the accepted training handout in TAP classes and employment courses at Military Transition Centers worldwide and is utilized in more than 100 military bases around the world. This publication is also the featured guide supporting the Certified Federal Job Search Trainer program for career counselors on the Ten Steps to a Federal Job.

CREATING YOUR HIGH SCHOOL RESUME 3rd Edition—Throughout this workbook, students will respond to straightforward questions about their skills and interests to help them build their resume section by section. Several case studies and samples show students firsthand how to focus, organize, write, format, and use their resumes. Students will learn how to format their resume using electronic tools, how to use the Web and email effectively for researching and finding contacts, and how to manage electronic resume files.

STUDENT'S FEDERAL CAREER GUIDE 2nd Edition—New release for the summer of 2011! This book is a must-buy for students, new graduates, young professionals, parents, college career centers, and career counselors. Details the winning 10-step process for going from the classroom to a federal job. Includes basics like our federal employment glossary, tips on salary negotiation, and a step-by-step guide to the behavior-based interview.

More information and secure online ordering:
www.resume-place.com
(888) 480-8265